THE LIFE OF THE WORLD TO COME

THE LIFE OF
THE
WORLD TO COME

Dom Anscar Vonier

2014

✠ Nihil Obstat.
Eduardus Mahoney, S.T.D.,
Censor Deputatus.

✠ Imprimatur.
Edm. Can. Surmont,
Vicarius Generalis.

Westminster
May 17, 1926.

The *Nihil Obstat* and *Imprimatur* are official declarations
that a book or pamphlet is free of doctrinal or moral error.
No implication is contained therein that those who have
granted the *Nihil Obstat* and the *Imprimatur* agree
with the content, opinions or statements expressed.

This book was originally published in 1926
by Benziger Bros.

Cover image: *The St. John Altarpiece,* detail,
Hans Memling, c. 1479

CONTENTS

FOREWORD

The essays which make the contents of this book have appeared at various times in the pages of our Abbey magazine, *Chimes*. Friends have asked me to gather them into book form; and I give them now as they first appeared. The reader must not expect a connected treatment of the doctrine of eternal life; yet most of the points known to Catholic theology in this matter of our eternal future are discussed—with some freedom, I admit—in the following pages. I may say, however, that the essay entitled "The Resurrection of the Body" is a careful and accurate study of that great mystery.

ANSCAR VONIER, O.S.B., Abbot of Buckfast.
BUCKFAST ABBEY, Feast of the Annunciation, 1926.

The Life of the
World to Come

I

THE WEALTH OF OUR HOPE

EVERY SUNDAY IN THE CREED we sing, as a final flourish, the words *et vitam venturi saeculi* ("and the life of the world to come"). In the musical setting of the great operatic Masses these last words of the Creed have indeed become something stupendous; melody is heaped upon melody, as if the composer could not leave the text, and ran back to it every time he had left it with a new and more ardent kiss than before.

The words merit such glorification; they express truly the mystery of eternal harmony; and no amount of melody here on earth will ever adequately render the depths of that great faith.

"I await the life of the world to come," says the believer; he expects a new life in a new world. He knows enough about his present life and the world in which it is spent. He is very tired of them both—the present life and the present world—so he sits down; and when you ask him why he is thus sitting by the roadside, he tells you that he is waiting for something; he says in the Creed: *expecto*, "I await," as he would expect or await somebody or something already on the road. He does not use the word *spero*, "I hope," but *expecto*, "I await," because the world to come, with its life, is on the road already, it is moving out of infinite distance, coming nearer every day, as stars and planets are said to be moving towards the earth from incalculable distances, yet with a surety and swiftness which make their coming into the horizon of our observation a matter of determined certainty.

The Christian is not only hopeful, then, of a better fate in some future existence, but he is more than that. Believing in all the articles of the Creed, and, of course, living up to them, he may indeed sit and await the chariot of God; it is sure to come his way; the world to come with its life will take him up as on a chariot of triumph. "The chariot of God is attended by ten thousands; thousands of them that rejoice" (Ps 67:18).

This, then, is the first profound thing, the first deep note of our theological thoughts; instead of saying that we hope to have eternal life, we are made to say that we await the life of the world to come. Hoping for something is profoundly different from awaiting something. You await a train; you hope for fine weather. A train is always sure to arrive; if you are early you sit down and feel the happiness of certainty. But if you are bent on pleasure your hope of a fine day has an element of disturbance; you are not quite, quite certain whether the fine weather will hold. Hope is a very different thing from expectation. There is in hope an element of uncertainty, a kind of struggle; we have to work ourselves up to it when we hope earnestly; expectation, waiting, is so easy; a child can do it; you never get fussy unless you fail in hope and begin to dread that after all the thing you want is not going to happen.

So, in the atmosphere of purely spiritual things, when we hope we do something more than to expect, to await something; we make an effort of the mind and heart; *spes est boni ardui*, "hope strains for what is difficult, arduous." The difficult thing is this, to possess now the life of God in our frail, poor souls, so much inclined to the life of sin. Incredible as it seems, in spite of all appearances to the contrary, yet through hope we feel confident that God's life is in us, that we are of the family of God, and that God comes out to us, down into our souls, to lift them up to Himself.

Hope has then for its object, not directly the life of the world to come, but the life of God in this world. We hope to lay hold on God through all the darkness of our mortal existence; we hope that through His grace we may never let Him go, that We shall persevere in His love to the very end, that death will find us alive in Him. This is why hope is called a theological virtue: it has God for its object; not God in the distant future; no virtues are ever of the future, they are ever of the present hour. In hope we throw ourselves forward now, with a mighty effort, so as to seize God in spite of that other constant tendency of our fallen souls to retreat from God. If hope were only of future things it would be something less than faith and charity, which are essentially our better life now, this very moment.

But this great conquest of God once achieved, this great difficulty of our own pusillanimity once overcome, with the supernatural certainty in our hearts that God will never abandon us we compose ourselves into peaceful expectation; we await the life of the world to come as a most natural sequel: We await it as we await the resurrection of the dead, for such is the double expectation of the Creed: *et expecto resurrectionem mortuorum, et vitam venturi saeculi* ("and I expect the resurrection of the dead, and the life of the world to come.") It is clear that with regard to that great thing, the resurrection of the dead, we are merely in an attitude of expectancy; none of us can do anything to bring it about; it will come in the hour which the Father has not revealed to any creature. So with the life of the world to come. It is sure to come out of the treasury of God's omnipotence; it is sure to take us up, to carry us on the bosom of its waves of glory, if we are found worthy, if God is in us through faith and hope and charity.

Sanctity is a very practical thing, not a distant dream. A saint is a great being wherever he is; he has achieved the greatest of all victories before the day of eternity dawns; he has found God through the might of his hope whilst his soul is yet in his body. The life of the world to come is a mere result of the more essential victory, to possess God. For that he can wait, for the possession of God he cannot wait; if he waited he would not be a saint. The great conquest is to possess God; hope is the forward *élan* of the soul that rushes the obstacles that fence round, not God indeed, but the soul itself. When once the obstacles are rushed, when once God is attained, the conquering hero may sit in his tent and await the hour when he will be told the number of prisoners and the amount of booty. It would not be a practical thing in spiritual life to make an effort to seize the life of the world to come: the world to come is still far away; but it is a most practical achievement for the soul to leap forward towards God, who is just on the other side of that trench which sin and worldliness have dug about the soul. There is a deep note of wisdom in the melody of the *Credo* when we sing *expecto* instead of *spero* the life of the world to come.

The expression of the Creed, "life of the world to come," is a stroke of genius. It is so difficult for the human mind to find terms that will render truth adequately; even when we see a thing clearly, the chances are that we shall spoil our thought through a wrong word. No happier phrase was ever coined than the last sentence of the Nicene Creed. We all know at once what is meant when anyone speaks of the life of the present world. It would take a long time to enumerate all the things that constitute the life of this actual world where we have our being, but instinctively we see its main aspects; with our long experience of it we know at once what it is. Now the Creed uses a similar phrase for a thing infinitely higher; it speaks of the life of the world to come with the same ease as we speak of the life of this present world. The expression sums up everything conceivable that can make creatures permanently happy. If the Creed had made us say that we expect heaven, or beatific vision, or eternal happiness, it would have curtailed the extent of our expectation; even the words "eternal happiness" imply a certain limitation, as happiness is a state of soul, whilst "life of the world to come" means every conceivable element, both internal and external, for man or angel. It means a new world and an existence in keeping with it.

There is a fairy-like richness in the expression "life of the world to come." We can read into it any meaning compatible with God's boundless sanctity; it gives full scope to our imagination, our reason, our sentiment; the man with the greatest powers of phantasy and the keenest intellect will be the one to say the truest things of the life of the world to come, because he will be able to conjure up vision which the smaller mind could never originate. Let him boundlessly enlarge the idea of a world and the idea of life, and he will not be far wrong in anything he may say about the Christian's great expectation. The glorious phrase of the Creed is the seed that produced Dante's *Paradiso*.

The main thing for us to do, in order not to commit any gaucherie in our mental picturings of the life of the world to come, is to find out what are the true and what are the false longings of our nature. If I were such a discerner of my own spirit as to see at a glance which longings of my heart are merely temporary, merely provisional, merely accidental, then I could, with great clearness, see into the world to come; for true, permanent, deep-rooted longings would be my best guide for my own Paradiso, they would be better guides than Beatrice herself. In every case it would be sufficient for me to take each individual longing, appertaining to the unspoiled, the permanent part of my nature, and to say to it: "Be of good heart because thou wilt have thy fill in the world to come, thou wilt be part of the life of the world to come." " Blessed are they that hunger and thirst after justice: for they shall have their fill" (Matt 5:6).

The life of the world to come is above all and before all the true life of the present world made eternal, immortal, carried to its highest potentialities. The difficulty lies in discernment between true, and illusory life, between the abnormal yearnings of a fallen nature, and the steady aspirations of the sound spirit in man.

Even grave theology may speak in parables: Two men went out into the Australian desert to find gold; gold had been discovered, so it was rumored, at some unearthly distance from Bush civilization. The two men were stout-hearted enough, but rather deficient in the bump of locality; so they lost the direction they intended to follow, and very soon they were overtaken by the enemy that lies in wait for all men who thirst for gold—the thirst for water. But the two men succumbed unequally. One of the two, a monosyllabic man, kept his parched tongue firmly clinging to the roof of his mouth; the other, a verbose Celt, gave full expression to his ravings. "Oh for a bottle of water!" For a bottle of water he would give his

kingdom if he were ever made a king; for a bottle of water he would give
all the gold of Australia, above and below surface; for a bottle of water he
would give his very soul. Happily he did not say to whom he would give
his soul in exchange for a bottle of water; but in his mad thirst he was ready
for any bargain.

Fortunately my story need not end in a tragedy. The two men fell in
with others who carried water in abundance; they also found their gold,
and became prosperous and rich beyond their wildest dreams. Many years
passed. The man who would have given his soul for a bottle of water on the
day of his great thirst was celebrating his seventieth birthday, and expected
some unusual token of friendship from his old mate of the barren track,
who was now his colleague in the direction of immense enterprises, but
dwelt in a different city.

The gift came, a parcel directed in the well-known hand, evidently a
bottle. "I have it," exclaimed the jubilarian, "that old fox has succeeded in
getting for me a bottle of the famous wine which keeps the Emperor of
Austria in perpetual youth." But the bottle, when uncorked, discharged
nothing but stale water, such as might have come from the kitchen pump.
Our good Croesus was not as witty as he was wealthy. "Whatever does that
fellow mean by this silly joke?" was his rather ungrateful exclamation.

His letter to his old friend was barely civil. But the man whose appe-
tite had been so well under his control in the evil hour when the demon
of thirst had been upon them, in some mysterious way always came out
top in wit and prudence during the long partnership of the two pioneers.
He wrote back to the indignant septuagenarian a homily full of wisdom,
begging him to remember what he had once said of a bottle of water, and
inviting him to consider the improvement of their respective fortunes, how
their desires had taken such different turns, and how their appetites were
gratified in a way so vastly more exalted. The bottle of water, arriving on
the top wave of complete satisfaction of all human desires, was intended as
the highest gratification on so full a day, the remembrance of the immense
improvement of their condition.

The moral of my parable is as clear as the lesson to be derived from an Aesopian fable. Desires, wishes, longings, here on earth, on the stony desert of life, are very relative, very casual; we hardly know what we truly desire. Things for which at one time we are willing to barter our souls become stale, insipid, when circumstances alter. This difficulty in finding out man's real, unalterable desires, in reaching the very fountain-head of man's longing, is the main obstacle to our survey of the life that is to be in the world to come. But before my next installment, by dint of hard thinking, I hope I shall have been able to disentangle some true desires out of the infinitude of our daily wishings; for if it is a fairy's privilege to grant our daily wishes, it is a theologian's mission to promise the accomplishment of permanent aspirations in *vita venturi saeculi*.

II

OUR TRUE ASPIRATION

ONE DAY OUR LORD went into the house of one of the chief of the Pharisees on the Sabbath, to a repast which, no doubt, had been prepared in His honor. Our Lord hated the pharisaical mind most wholeheartedly; the hypocritical self-sufficiency of the sect was most nauseous to His beautiful, upright spirit; yet He moved with the greatest ease and courtesy among the very men whose whole spiritual temperament was so alien to His own. So on this occasion, though He was the guest, and though He knew himself to be watched, He spoke with the freedom of a king who has honored the table of an obedient courtier:

> When thou makest a dinner or a supper, call not thy friends, nor thy brethren, nor thy kinsmen, nor thy neighbours who are rich; lest perhaps they also invite thee again, and recompense be made to thee. But when thou makest a feast, call the poor, the maimed, the lame and the blind. And thou shalt be blessed, because they have not wherewith to make thee recompense: for recompense shall be made thee at the resurrection of the just. When one of them that sat at table with him had heard these things, he said to him: Blessed is he that shall eat bread in the kingdom of God (LUKE 14:12-15).

It is a prudent rule in Gospel interpretation always to follow the more kindly hypothesis, and to think well of the men that surrounded our Lord's person till their ill-will and wickedness be proven facts. So we ought to attach as good a meaning as possible to the mental effort made by the worthy man who was Christ's fellow-guest on that occasion. Evidently he wanted to add something fitting to Christ's words on the recompense to be given in the life of the world to come, "at the resurrection of the just."

Yet I cannot but surmise that the good man, with all his kind nature, did not soar very high in his desires; he was dreaming of an immense banquet, and to sit at that banquet in the kingdom of God was to him the limit of blessedness. Evidently he was not a Sadducee, one of those who said that there was no resurrection, no life of the world to come; he was a believer in the great future, but his faith, a true ray of light from heaven, was badly deflected as it entered the dense medium of his carnal mind. He had listened to Christ s exposition of the doctrine of recompense in the resurrection of the just. It was white, unrefracted light, straight from the mind of the Son of God. But as the ray was received by the crude intelligence of Christ's fellow-guest, it suffered a sad refraction. The reward at the resurrection of the just became for that simple man a glorified banquet, something surpassing the repast of which he was partaking at the time.

Man has always behaved mentally as did Christ's fellow-guest on that day. Very rarely has man given up belief in the world to come. The light of that faith comes to him from permanent constellations of his firmament, not from occasional meteors. We cannot trace the way in which the light travels to him and strikes upon the eye of his mind. This perception that there is life in the world to come, is God's most enduring gift to mankind, as perpetual as the order and harmony of the heavenly constellations. Men do not differ much about this fundamental belief; very few men, if any, are entirely without it; but they differ greatly in the mode in which they conceive the life of the world to come. Yet we may consider this to be only a minor spiritual misfortune. If I am told by a simple-minded shepherd, whose terrestrial abode is a dilapidated cottage on England's southern moor, that there is no happiness for him, either in this world or the next, without lambs and sheep, I feel no special calling to undeceive him, to coerce him into a dogmatic denial of the survival of the tribe of sheep in the world to come. Nor shall I ever frown at the private belief of some dear old soul whose vision of heaven is, after all, nothing but a glorified aviary.

The one thing that matters for mankind in general is a living belief in a future life, and a real, healthy terror of missing its good things through deliberate acts. I do not think that there is any real propensity in man's mind, even in its darkest periods, to project into the life of the world to come his actual, sinful enjoyments, his crimes, and his dark thoughts. Even for the most degraded there is something holy in the Hereafter; and, by a cunning piece of dexterity on the part of the human conscience, the pleasures of the world to come are always supposed to be lawful pleasures.

Not to look forward to another life is an unmitigated evil always, and at all times. Let us condemn it from the housetop; let us call such an absence of all hope man's greatest degradation. At the same time let us be careful to distinguish the gold of hopefulness in man's heart from the dross of vulgarity in man's imagination. One may hope for a future life, and yet be sadly deficient in imagination or visual power to picture that life. So we find Christ turning to good account His interlocutor's well-meant repartee as to the blessedness of eating bread in the kingdom of God.

The parable of the great supper is our Lord's rejoinder to the interrupter of His discourse on the recompense at the resurrection of the just. The parable, so much quoted in spiritual life, is addressed directly to that man. "But he said to him: A certain man made a great supper and invited many." The beeves and the fatlings are killed, and all things are ready; Christ improves on the vision of the guest; He lets him have more than he dreams of. What does it really matter? The one thing that is so terribly distressing is that the men who are invited do not come, that they all go their own way, that in their eagerness for the goods of the passing hour they despise the invitation to the distant banquet.

When we were children we had a most lively belief in the existence of heaven. Baptism is called by the early Fathers, and in fact by the Apostles themselves, the Illumination. In baptism the soul is illumined; its eyes are opened to the heavenly constellations. Small wonder, then, to find our Catholic children endowed with so keen a sense of the existence of the world to come. It is certainly a supernatural, a divine gift, that faith in heaven we find in the Catholic infant. Yet the heaven we dreamed of in our own dear childhood was of a very subjective nature indeed. We applied to our happy childish experience that power of magnifying that makes childhood one continuous enthusiasm; we magnified the beautiful things we had seen, and called our efforts heaven. The glories of the parish church, with its gilded saints, its lofty windows, its ceilings of incomprehensible color scheme, its odor of incense, even the priest in his wonderful integuments at the altar, things seen with awe, and endlessly enlarged by deep cogitation—such were perhaps the main elements of our own heavenly vision at an age when to keep quiet in church was heroic goodness.

No doubt there was also at work, even at that early period, the process of elimination and negation which is such an important function in mature theology. We eliminated from our heaven the cold hands and feet that made prayer so restless in the unheated church on Christmas night, or on the day when the three Kings were seen with crowns on their heads near the altar. Perhaps we even dismissed from our heaven the presence of the old folks whose voice, when praying aloud, sounded more like a scolding. Yet our heaven was there, on the retina of our childish mind, and with the help of imaginative powers, both positive and negative, our truly divine and heavenly infused faith produced deep effects in our young souls and made us into brothers of the angels.

It would seem, then, as if the Christian belief in the life of the world to come were of all the articles of the Creed the one whose objective reality remains a matter of freedom for individual minds more than would be allowed in any other province of Catholic dogma. A desire for a life in a world to come is for the soul of greater importance than a precision of knowledge as to the nature of that life. Few men, comparatively, are capable of such knowledge, but all men are expected to harbor in their hearts the great desire to expect something that is in every way better than the life here on earth.

This motherly indulgence of the Church of God in smiling benignly at each notion that comes to one of her children when her family begins to babble of the life of the world to come is in strong contrast with her theological imperiousness in other matters. "Eye hath not seen, nor ear heard: neither hath it entered into the heart of man, what things God hath prepared for them that love him" (1 COR 2:9). Holy Mother the Church seems to be repeating to herself words such as these when we, her children, give full play to our inventive genius in our talks on heaven. She knows that we cannot go dangerously wrong in theology whilst there is in our heart a sincere desire for the great life in the world to come. In most other dogmatic matters we should be pulled up at a much earlier period in the workings of our individual minds.

Some reader with a good memory will begin at this point to wonder whether all this philosophy is not an effort on my part to escape from the fulfillment of the rash promise made in the former article to find out which are the permanent desires of the human heart, in opposition to the transient, superficial wishes. I said then that the best way to find out what heaven really means to us is to diagnose human nature, to see what human nature desires with truth and constancy, the life of the world to come being above all the realization of such desires.

The considerations that have occupied us so far seem to favor a kind of benign agnosticism in our mental attitude towards the nature of the great future life. But here I may protest. Nothing is further from my habitual theological outlook than mild skepticism. I know where truth is to be found, and I know, too, that there are many souls that are thirsting for the real facts of a theological case. "To the Greeks and to the barbarians, to the wise and to the unwise, I am a debtor" (ROM 1:14) Before giving satisfaction to the Greek, who is devoid of imagination, and to the wise thinker, who dislikes mere symbols, I thought I ought to show how there can be the real supernatural faith in a future life in the heart of the naïve barbarian, whose mind is incapable of higher speculations, and also in the heart of children who, more than any other class of human beings, project—an awful word for an infant—their own dear minds into everything outside themselves.

So let us approach the Greek and the wise thinker, and let us ask of them what they consider to be the permanent desires of human nature. After making my promise to discover man's permanent longings of heart I felt rather despondent; I thought I had undertaken too much. But Providence is kind. So Christmas brought me, along with its pictures of the Divine Infant, a wonderful book—Christmas is always a lady bountiful—a volume of the Hibbert Lectures, by Professor Wicksteed, on Reactions between Dogma and Philosophy. Plato himself could not be more of a Greek nor Aristotle more of a wise man than are the men who deliver the Hibbert Lectures. Dr. Wicksteed, for one, in the thrilling and substantial volume, whose very sight gladdened my heart on Christmas morning, undertakes to show what St. Thomas Aquinas made of Christian thought.

Lecture the second is on "The Goal Postulated by Human Nature"; all I need do is to transcribe his words. True and permanent human desires cannot be anything else except a wish to reach that goal; by showing me the true nature of my desires the Hibbert Lecturer, be it said with thankfulness, shows, if not the way to heaven, at least heaven's position. "Aristotle's Teleology," says our lecturer,

> or belief in the goalfulness of nature, carries with it the principle that things can only be understood by considering what it is they are making for. The potentialities of the acorn can only be read in the light of the actualized functionings of the oak. But this principle … becomes in Aquinas a defined and compact conviction that since all things proceed from the will of God, and the will is always directed to an end, all things are directed by God to the attainment of some "finis" which is connatural to them, and in the attainment of

which they rest and find their good. Hence, if we can discover what is the specific "good" connatural to any creature, we have hereby discovered the goal which it is naturally destined to attain. … Now, the conception, however vague, of a conclusive and comprehensive satisfaction of attainment, a definite realization of happiness, bliss, or whatever we may name the supreme object of desire, is obviously implanted in the human mind. … Consideration will show that those philosophers who have sought this conclusive blessedness in anything that man shares with the brutes have not really been contemplating human blessedness at all, for that must be related to the distinctive element in man which makes him human. And this cannot be found elsewhere than in his intellectual nature. … It is, then, in the life of the intelligence that the specifically human life is found, and so we must look for the Specific human blessedness also in some act, possession, or experience of the intelligence and not of the senses.

I feel sure I have quoted now enough Greek wisdom to satisfy most of my readers. As the suspension marks in the above paragraph proclaim, I have not quoted *in extenso* ("extensively"), but just sucked the honey out of an immense sunflower. The nectar of it all is the very limpid truth that, whatever we may do, we cannot be happy except in the exercise of the intellectual portion of our nature, and consequently our true, permanent desires and wishes are found in the intellectual sphere of our persons. And to those desires, upon my honor as a theologian, I promise full and complete satisfaction in the life of the world to come.

If any legitimate desire that appertains to our intellectual life were not to have its fill, sooner or later, what Dr. Wicksteed calls so aptly the "goalfulness" of our human nature would be wrong—a most alarming supposition indeed, as such misfiring of our intellectual aspirations would simply mean this, that God has launched us into the realms of hopefulness, but does not mean to grant the goal towards which He is driving us. Such an hypothesis is a *reductio ad absurdum*, a thing of utter silliness.

So the only labor that remains to the theologian in his effort to make the spiritual chart of the life of the world to come is to enumerate man's truly intellectual activities and desires. Between this chart or map and the future reality there will be the same proportion which is found to exist between the map that hangs on a wall and represents a continent, and the continent itself. Even a child knows that a map of America and the American continent are two different propositions altogether. Yet there is a real family resemblance between the two things otherwise so disproportionately different. Anything we may say now of man's intellectual life is truly to be found in the life of the world to come, but on a scale that is almost in proportion of the infinite to the finite, "For God does not give the Spirit by measure" (JOHN 3:34). The realization of our spiritual desires in heaven has no measure. Our Lord gives us a description of the divine scale of fulfillment in heaven: "Good measure and pressed down and shaken together and running over shall they give into your bosom" (LUKE 6:38). Yet the bosom into which all that measureless Wealth will be poured some day is our natural intellectual life, into every corner of which the divine recompense will be poured by God's mighty palm. All our dormant intellectual potentialities, perhaps now unknown to us, or known only subconsciously, will be shaken mightily by the Holy Ghost, so as to enlarge their receptiveness, and make them into immense vessels of light.

But here I perceive a critical expression on the countenance of my readers. The question they are asking me is a perplexing one: "Have you really taken us one step further with all this theology? You promised to disentangle the true desires of man's nature from his passing wishes; by saying that the desires of man's intellectual sphere of life are true desires that will never fail him, you have only taken us from one dark room to another. What, then, are those intellectual longings within us which have so grand a future? Do we desire anything intellectually? If so, when does it happen, what are the signs of such aspirations?"

I will admit that here lies the crux of the whole matter. Whatever is in us, or is desired by us intellectually, will be made into eternal life by God's grace. All other things will fall away as not truly belonging to our nature, like so many heavy garments which are bearable only in the sharp cold of winter. But what is the intellectual in us? How far does the province of intellectual life extend in our human life?

My Hibbert lecturer does not desert me here. In broad outlines he draws for me the chart of that permanent element in man which we are so anxious to have separated from the merely sensuous:

> The intelligence, therefore, is the organ, and the sole organ, of all aesthetic and normal perceptions, as well as of those that we should in our narrowed modern use of the word describe as "intellectual." The intelligence, in short, is the faculty that recognizes not only truth, but beauty and goodness, as making whatever they characterize desirable. ... We must enlarge our conception of "intelligence" so as to make it include the organ of spiritual perception of every kind.

Here, again, I have been the busy bee gathering one drop of most precious honey from Hymettus. The wise words I quote here allow me to put the matter as follows: whatever is aesthetical and exalted is the region of the intellect; whatever is lower than the aesthetical is the region of the brute. Aesthetics are truly the line of demarcation. There may be greater things than the aesthetical things in man; but aesthetical things are certainly permanent, and whatever in man does not reach that height, let the worms devour it in our graves. If our bodies belong to the life of the world to come, they must at least satisfy this exigency, they must be part of the heavenly aesthetics. Perhaps they may do work that is still more spiritual, but unless they give satisfaction to the divine aesthete, Christ, the all-beautiful, they can never take part in the resurrection of the just.

To be "lovers of beautifulness" (ECCL 44:6) is the badge of all those who move heavenwards. This love is the first thing in man that can be made use of by God when He makes man into an eternal thing. The craving that consumes your soul like fire, has it truly the authentic stamp, the mark of beautifulness? Well, then, with God's grace you will receive your fill in heaven; your desire is like a chaste bosom into which will be poured a measure of satisfaction that is good, well-shaken, pressed down, flowing over. If, on the contrary, there is something ugly in your great hunger and thirst, something which no artist, human or angelic, could love, then for God's sake do not ask me to promise that such a craving will find satisfaction on an immense scale, or on any scale at all for the matter of that, in the world to come. I may smile at your simplicity if you persist in such a demand, but I could never encourage you in your expectation.

Most unaesthetical indeed was that theological conundrum proposed by a group of Sadducees to Christ, the case of the woman who had buried seven husbands, all brothers, and about whom the Sadducees—"who deny that there is any resurrection" (MATT 22:23)—feigned such concern; they wanted to know which of the seven brothers would have her for his wife in the world to come, as she had been the wife of each one of them in this world. Our Lord, though He had to deal with coarse men, let them down gently, but not without uncomplimentary allusion to their lack of mental vision:

> You err, not knowing the Scriptures nor the power of God. For in
> the resurrection they shall neither marry nor be married, but shall
> be as the angels of God in heaven (MATT 22:29).

The Sadducces thought they had a good argument against the life of the world to come, because in their vulgar imaginations another life must be essentially a literal prolongation of the things of this life. Our Lord points out to them the power of God as the discriminating agent that will separate what is angelic in man from what is sensuous. Such spiritual love as there had been in the very cumulative matrimonial ties of the woman in the hypothesis of the Sadducees will survive in the comprehensive love of angelic life. As for the claims of the seven husbands on the one lady, such claims being intrinsically a transient phase in their lives—*abeant quo libuerint* ("They are free; let them go.").

III

Self in Eternal Life

I T IS ONE OF THE COMMONEST wishes of our naïve human nature to desire to be somebody else or even something else. A child wishes himself to be a bird, an unsuccessful middle-aged man wishes himself to be the very person of a prosperous rival. We all have a share in various degrees in the mental infirmity attributed to a notorious sovereign personage of whom it was said that he wanted to play the leading part in any function he condescended to grace with his presence; at a wedding he wished to be the bride, and at a funeral desired to be the corpse.

St. Thomas Aquinas happens to deal with this form of human longing more than once, even when he is in his gravest moods, and invariably he says of it that there is no sincerity, no truth in such a desire; none of us ever mean to be anything except ourselves; in fact, St. Thomas says emphatically that it is quite impossible for any being, that can feel and desire, to wish to be anything except itself: it cannot even wish to be a higher being than itself. It is a mere play of our imagination when we fancy that we should like to be, as the saying is, in somebody else's shoes, or, better still, in somebody else's skin. In truth and reality we never have such a desire. We want to be ourselves everywhere, always, under all circumstances, in time and in eternity.

A little exact thought will help my reader to see through the inanity and insincerity of his own longings whenever he wishes himself to be an archangel, or even something less ambitious; you could not be an archangel without ceasing to be a human being; you could not become a happy, unfettered nightingale without losing all that makes your personality. Therefore, whether you mean to be a higher being than you are now, or a lower one, the essential, unavoidable requisite of such ascent or descent is this, that you should cease to be what you are. Annihilation of your own present self is the first condition of being something else or somebody else. Now you cannot wish, and you do not wish, your own annihilation simply because, through the fact of having a great longing, you want to be, to exist, to enjoy yourself, either as a nightingale or an archangel. For if you were annihilated there would not be the faintest link between you and the new being, if a new being were to appear in your stead. Your annihilation would wipe you out completely—desires, claims, rights, and all—and there would be no more of you in the hypothetical new being than if you had never existed. The nightingale or the archangel would not be your own self transformed, but they themselves, with not a vestige of memory or love of you.

It would be, indeed, a most tragic "take in" for you, if ever it went as far with you as annihilation. We simply cannot get away from our own persons; we are our own selves, and, what is more, we do not wish to be anything but our own selves in all our desires and expectations for time and beyond time. To fancy anything different is a clumsy maneuvering on the part of our imagination, an imitation of the Baron von Münchhausen, who thought he could climb up a tower or let himself down from a tower —- I don't remember which it was—by using his own hair, still firmly rooted on his head and twisted into a solid tress, as a rope. In the naïve phantasy I am describing we want to lift ourselves above ourselves, we want to let ourselves down below ourselves, but all along we cling to ourselves most tenaciously: we clutch our very being with grim determination, firmly resolved not to let it go.

So what we are really doing when we hug the aforesaid desires of being something else or somebody else is this: we want all the qualities and liberties and privileges of the beings whom we envy; we covet their place, their very natures; but, after all is said, we are the pivot of the whole transaction and prospective transformation. We think of coming back to our friends to surprise them in our new role, in our transformed state, to make them feel how wrong they were in thinking us hopeless failures. The present "I" is truly at the bottom of our heart, the connecting link between our present, unsatisfactory frame of mind and the glorious substitution of personality and role we may be dreaming of for our actual, humdrum existence. So also the imperial person of my tale wished to be himself the bride or the corpse just in anticipation of hearing the praises of himself as the bride and the eulogium of himself as the dead man, at his own royal breakfast table when the newspapers would be full of them. His persistent and assertive "Ego" was powerful enough to melt all those extraordinary attitudes into one subliminal element, his individual self.

Dear reader, do not think I am out to play with you to-day with all these taunts to that portion of your mind where fairy stories are born and thrive. I am in the very heart of my solemn subject, the life of the world to come. Open the second Epistle to the Corinthians at the fifth chapter, and you will at once forgive me for my lighter vein. There you will find the majesty of St. Paul lending immense weight and dignity to the very point which I have dared to illustrate, by way of contraries, with a Münchhausen legend. Says St. Paul:

> For we know, if our earthly house of this habitation be dissolved, that we have a building of God, a house not made with hands, eternal in heaven. For in this also we groan, desiring to be clothed upon with our habitation that is from heaven. Yet so that we be found clothed, not naked. For we also, who are in this tabernacle, do groan, being burdened; because we would not be unclothed, but clothed upon, that that which is mortal may be swallowed up by life (2 COR 5:1-4).

Here we have the Holy Ghost telling us the true way of desiring to be something or somebody else; for there is a genuine, sensible way of having the desires described at the beginning of the paragraph, as there is a false, silly way about them. But for my own theological justification I fix at once upon the words, "because we would not be unclothed, but clothed upon." St. Paul says in a metaphor what I said in metaphysical language. I used the term annihilation. St. Paul calls it being unclothed. He says, explaining man's desire for another life, that man is by very nature adverse to being stripped of his garment of life and existence; man does not cherish the notion of being reduced to nakedness in the ontological sense of the word; he wants to keep his garment of existence; all he wishes is this, that a new, a more beautiful garment should come down over his shoulders and cover the one that he already wears.

St. Paul speaks in the language of a poet the metaphysical truth that man never wishes to lose his present personality. When we come to examine our fondest hopes, when we come to analyze our most far-flung aspirations, it always comes to this, that we want to be "clothed upon," to wear over our own selves the garments of another state, the robes of higher beings, the glories of a more elevated grade of existence; it is always our present being which receives fresh ornaments, new splendors, "that that which is mortal may be swallowed up by life."

Lucifer, the greatest of God's creatures, is commonly said to have had the ambition of becoming God. St. Thomas shrewdly observes that this could not be taken literally:

> Even if it were possible for a creature to become God this would be against the creature's natural desire. Every being has its natural desire to keep its existence; now this existence would be lost if it were changed into another nature. Therefore it is impossible that a lower angel should desire to be equal to God.[1]

---

1   St. Thomas Aquinas, *Summa Theologiae*, I-II, q. 63, a. 3

What Lucifer desired was to have in his own person the liberty and independence of Godhead Itself.

I feel that I am doing my patient reader a great service through this reiteration of the fact that we can never desire to be anything or anybody else except ourselves. It is certainly strange how with many people there seems to be a kind of duality of persons, looking on themselves in their heavenly attire—we all hope to be found in heaven one day—as something quite distinct from the persons that wear the workaday costume here on earth.

> For I know that my Redeemer liveth, and in the last day I shall rise out of the earth. And I shall be clothed again with my skin: and in my flesh I shall see my God. Whom I myself shall see, and my eyes shall behold; and not another (JOB 19:25).

Were there in the days of Job, in the land of Hus, people of such dreamy theology as to provoke this ardent profession of Job's faith; or are vague, undefined longings to be somebody else, somebody better, in another world, the property of our own misty heavens and our mistier intellects?

St. Francis of Assisi was often in contact with a man who was a public sinner, yet the dear Saint treated that man with unusual reverence and courtesy. The reason of this preference was to be found in an assurance received from God that the man would be in heaven one day, through death-bed repentance. Is there anything more overpowering than the truth contained in Job's fervent cry, "I myself shall see, and my eyes shall behold, and not another"? Yet to bring this home, each one to himself, constitutes the difference between a vague dream about the world to come and an ardent love of our true home. Survival, then, of our personality, uninterrupted continuance of our central existence is for us the key to the life of the world to come.

This life of the world to come is called by St. Paul a house: "We have a building of God, a house not made with hands, eternal in heaven" (2 COR 5:1). Or, again, he describes it as a garment: "For in this also we groan, desiring to be clothed upon with our habitation that is from heaven" (2

Cor 5:2). It is a wonderful play in metaphors, but also a wonderful way of impressing upon the mind the double truth that matters above all other truths, that we shall be new people in the life of the world to come, yet the same people. A house is pulled down, a new house is built up over the head, as it were, of an undisturbed personality, undisturbed in its identity. A garment descends from heaven, not on one who is stripped of all things, God forbid! "Yet so that we be found clothed, not naked" (2 Cor 5:3). It is an upper garment that comes to us out of God's wardrobes; we are already covered with the merits of our personal life which remain.

The house that is pulled down about our ears is "our house of this earthly habitation," our mortal, bodily life, of mud walls and ruinous roofs. Yet it was a habitation; it must be replaced. St. Paul is very insistent on this feature of God's husbandry:

> For we know if our house of this habitation be dissolved, that we have a building of God, a house not made with hands, eternal in the heavens (2 Cor 5:1).

Do any of my readers remember my doctrine of the permanence of our earthly wishes in the life of the world to come? I said that all things that are aesthetical, beautiful, will remain; all things that fall short of this rule will not be given back to us in the world to come, however much we may cling to them.

St. Paul comes to us with a plan of a new house. God is the Architect; the house is not made with hands; it is eternal. Yet it is a house, it is to replace another house, "our earthly house of this habitation." The tumble-down cottage goes, but our fondest dreams of a perfect dwelling are outstripped by the achievement of the heavenly Architect in building on the same foundation.

The closer we keep to the instincts and innate desires of our nature, the safer is our orthodoxy. We shall be most accurate theologically if we are close observers of man's true life. The resurrection of our bodies is the acid test of our orthodoxy; no man is truly a Christian in his intellect unless he believes firmly that in the world to come mankind will be, not a multitude of ghosts, however glorious, but a race with a distinct human personality, composed of soul and body, as here on earth. The difference will not be in our constitution, but in our qualifications: we shall be constituted then, as we are constituted now, of soul and body; but soul and body will possess qualities almost infinitely more perfect than are the charms and attractions of the best born and highest born among men. But this high belief, which I call the acid test of orthodoxy, is truly consonant with man's innate repugnance to losing his identity, his personality.

People who say that they want eternal life without the encumbrance of a body are sadly deluded by their imagination. What do they know of life, of existence, as separated from their body? Have they ever lived, were it only for an infinitesimal instant, a life that is not in the body, of the body, through the body? If they were good searchers of their own thoughts, expert analyzers of their own nature, they would have found out long ago that the moments of their highest and purest activities were the high-water mark of their best bodily powers. They never felt their souls, they never acted as spirits. When they ask for a life into which the body does not enter, they do not know what they are asking for.

It is not in man's power truly to desiderate a life in which the body does not have its share, because no one can truly have a desire of a thing which is absolutely beyond his experience and comprehension. Is there any man, outside a lunatic asylum, who wishes for himself such existence as that of a possible race of beings in the planet Jupiter? As he knows nothing of the conditions of such an existence, the sane man cannot feel any enthusiasm for it.

We do not desire to be angels, as I said already, though all we who are pious desire to be like the angels, which is a very different sort of desire. So we cannot wish to be souls without a body, though we may desire for our body many of the qualities possessed by the soul. What we all thirst for is the continuance of our own selves, as we know ourselves, of our individual life; and the dogma of the great resurrection tallies perfectly well with all our philosophy, theoretical and practical, on human personality.

There is, however, One who can do the thing from which nature recoils: the Holy Ghost can inspire the Christian with the desire "to be absent rather from the body and to be present with the Lord" (2 COR 5:8). The Christian has aspirations which could never spring from the human heart untouched by the Holy Ghost. Christ is dearer to the Christian than natural life, "knowing that while we are in the body we are absent from the Lord" (2 COR 5:6). We do not exactly desire a state of disembodiment for our soul, but we long to be near Christ. This is best done before the day of the general resurrection, through the separation of the soul from the body. So we actually dare to do what nature, unaided by the Holy Ghost, could never do: We desire death, we desire the absence of our soul from our body:

> Now he that maketh us for this very thing is God, who hath given us the pledge of the Spirit. Therefore having always confidence ... we are confident and have a good will to be absent rather from the body and to be present with the Lord (2 COR 5:5-8).

But who does not see how this Christian privilege makes human grammar almost impossible? "We" here stands for the whole Christian, the person who, whether absent or present, "labors to please the Lord" (2 COR 5:9). The labor is of soul and body. Yet these same "we" again are absent from a portion of themselves, to be present with the Lord; and they are also absent from the Lord, to be present to themselves. What seems a contradiction to nature is harmonized through a higher element, the divine Spirit, who will make it possible for the Christian thus to duplicate his person, because, through the Holy Ghost, he is more in Christ than in himself. But there will be the full, the undivided presence of man with Christ in His glory, the all-comprehensive "we" at the resurrection:

> Then we ... shall be taken up ... in the clouds to meet Christ, into the air: and so shall we be always with the Lord (1 THESS 4:16).

IV

NOONTIDE BRIGHTNESS OF MIND

THERE IS NO SURER SIGN of decadence than an aversion for knowledge. Not to want to know is the beginning of brutalization in man. A passion for knowledge is the surest sign of a healthy mental constitution, whilst listlessness and indifference for the bright things of the intellect argues more than mental paralysis: it is a positive depravity of the heart; the heart has become heavy through the things of the senses, and it loathes the effort which is implied in all true knowledge.

Judged by this standard, our present generation may appear to some of us as being very near unto salvation. Was there ever a greater effort in the field of knowledge than in our own days? Did men ever attach more value to knowledge than they do now? It is happily not my mission to sit in judgement on my fellow-men. Nothing would please me more than the discovery that a great thirst for knowledge is truly discernible amongst the men and women of the present generation. With such a thirst none of them can be far from the kingdom of God, and the harvest of souls is sure to be a record crop.

There are, however, some alarming signs that this thirst is not a healthy desire for the waters of the spirit, but only the fevered craving of a sick man. Was there ever a greater and more outspoken dislike of doctrine than in our own days? This is a question to be asked in conjunction with the rather complacent questions I put a moment ago into the mouth of an unseen interlocutor. If our society is conspicuous for its appreciation of knowledge, it is not less remarkable for its dislike of doctrine or dogma.

Perhaps an apologist of modern life has a ready answer: he will say that aversion for doctrine is the very thing you will find in a man who thirsts for knowledge. Doctrine fetters the mind and cramps the flight of the intellect towards the regions of pure knowledge. If dislike of doctrine and dogma—and I do not here exclude Catholic doctrine and dogma—were accompanied in our moderns by an intense eagerness to find out things high and divine, by an effort to meet with truth as great as is their energy in driving out doctrine and dogma, one would not be greatly alarmed. A Catholic would just watch the dogma destroyer, as from a safe boat one watches the too-eager traveler, who, thinking the ship too slow, jumped into the rough sea in order to reach the shore an hour before the landing of the boat. One would look on such an effort almost good-naturedly, in spite of the overhanging peril. The impatient swimmer will soon be glad to find himself in the boat again; he had been quite out in his reckoning about the distance and about his own physical capacity.

Unfortunately we do not seem to be able to lay such balm to our hearts when we see the persistent aversion for Catholic doctrine in society. There is nowhere noticeable that compensating effort I have just described. The effort to drive out dogma leaves no energy behind to find out things divine. It is not a passion for knowledge, but a positive dislike of knowledge that is at the root of all aversion for doctrine.

How, then, shall we appraise the countless millions that are spent on education: are they not the measure of our thirst for knowledge? Let us not be hard on anyone, but let us admit without any further grudge that the tax-gatherer's hand is heavy on all of us for this very thing, the acquisition of knowledge by man. All men want to know something, all men are asking for knowledge of some kind, and if any man throws ridicule on the old scholastic contention that a desire for knowledge is man's most persistent natural craving, I will ask him to peruse the balance-sheet of the Board of Education. We may consider the modern dislike for doctrine and the modern craving for science as one of those human anomalies of which the history of mankind is so full, and without further diagnosing this mental portent we may take it for granted that the love of knowledge is the last thing to leave any man in his downward course. When doctrine becomes to his diseased mind a kind of bugbear, he clutches all the more tenaciously at what he calls science, which, after all, is merely doctrine on a small and limited scale. Like a bird frightened by some empty sound, man flies away from the cedars of doctrine and hides under the hyssop of science.

Knowledge, more knowledge, knowledge without any limit, such is truly the view Catholic theology takes of man's destiny. Man is born to know, as the beast of burden is born to labor. There may be temporary obstacles to that flood of knowledge which in God's plan of the universe is meant to reach man's soul; but the obstacles are not so much hindrances to the advent of that flood as guidances to its course; in God's providence knowledge comes to man gradually, wave after wave, but a day will come when man will be fit for all knowledge, and that day is the first day in the life of the world to come.

Our theological treatises, of the more technical kind, on the life of the world to come, are practically nothing else than philosophical researches on man's capacity for knowing. The theologian best fitted to write wise things on the great life to come is the thinker who sees deepest into the latent capabilities of the human intellect. Such a man we follow as our master, and whosoever has a poor opinion of the resourcefulness of the human mind ought to be forbidden to treat of eternal life; from such a pen we could never get more than a child's fairy tales.

Anyone who has been through a course of Catholic theology will remember the hot summer days that preceded the great ordeal of public examinations, when he sought for a shady nook where he could, in coolness of body and mind, grapple victoriously with the great Thomistic distinction of *species impressa* ("impressed form or species") and *species expressa* ("expressed form or species)", and of the more arduous *verbum mentis* ("mental word"), all of them wonderful definitions of the mental capabilities of man, lying at the base of the gigantic edifice of knowledge that will be man's inheritance in the life to come. For his comfort the much exhausted student in theology is told that by means of the three great realities implied in the aforesaid definitions, his intellect, one day, if he but die in the grace of God, will practically become omniscient; the whole mighty universe will one day be reflected in his mind, as in a mirror, and he himself will find it possible to express that universe to himself and to other minds. Many a student has been tempted to look upon his present labors as upon idle and wasted efforts, being mindful that such an inheritance of knowledge would be his one day without any such effort. Happily the dread of the public examination keeps him from sinking into that mental slothfulness which would be for him the surest road to the loss of that heavenly wealth of knowledge and light which is the reward of all mortal struggle.

Our theologians are so profoundly imbued with the idea that life in the world to come is all knowledge that the task they set themselves is to find out whether there is really anything which man will not be capable of knowing. Their united labors have resulted in this one conclusion, that all we can say is this, that man, and, for the matter of that, any other created Intellect, will never be able to know God as God knows Himself; it is the only limit they admit for the possibilities of the human mind in the happy world to come.

They do not say that man will not know God; what they say is that man could never know God as God knows Himself. Our theology has no other reservations. Everything else is possible. We do not maintain that all human beings in heaven will stop short just of that last limit; the measure of knowledge goes by the sanctity of our life here on earth, and our lives differ greatly in merit and perfection. But so far I am concerned only with the general principle of our mental powers in the glorious state of eternal salvation, and, taking the state merely from its generic characteristics, every human soul could have knowledge of such extent as to make the aforesaid reservation the only necessary limit.

Nothing is brought home to us so insistently as the enormous disproportion in the present life between reality and our knowledge of reality. Wherever we look we see an infinitude of things of whose nature and workings we are deeply ignorant. Our minds in our present state are almost infinitely smaller than the world of realities that surrounds them. Could there be a reversal of roles in this matter? Could it ever be that our minds should be greater than created reality? Could it ever be that we should know more than what is, than what exists, and that the existing things should be as a handful to our enlarged minds? Could we truly hope for such superiority of mind?

Our theologians have no hesitation in saying that such a reversal of situations will take place in the life of the world to come. The blessed in heaven will look upon all things as from above, not from below them. The only reality that will be above them is God, and such qualities as are directly divine in the other elect. It is in this wonderful superiority of knowledge that we shall find the true meaning of the constantly reiterated assertion that the elect will occupy thrones of glory, that they will be princes in the house of God, that they will be exalted above all measure.

Knowledge, and the degrees of knowledge, are the true substance and inwardness of all the wonderful symbolism of our Scriptures in this matter of the life in the world to come. A giant in heaven is a vast mind, and a ruler is one whose intellect dominates the whole mighty field of created realities. The powers, the principalities, the thrones, the dominations in heavenly places are degrees of intellect and modes of apprehending all truth:

> Thou shalt no more have the sun for thy light by day, neither shall the brightness of the moon enlighten thee: but the Lord shall be unto thee for an everlasting light, and thy God for thy glory. Thy sun shall go down no more and thy moon shall not decrease. For the Lord shall be unto thee for an everlasting light: and the days of

thy mourning shall be ended. And thy people shall be all just: they shall inherit the land for ever, the branch of my planting, the work of my hand, to glorify me. The least shall become a thousand, and a little one a most strong nation: I, the Lord, will suddenly do this thing in its time (Isa 60 19-22).

In this canticle the seer truly sings a reversal of roles, of attitudes, of ways of illumination, in the life of the world to come. The sun and the moon will behave in a way contrary to their very character, to their natural laws; the least of the elect will have the wisdom of a thousand wise heads, and a nation's accumulated lore will be as nothing when compared with the power of vision of a little one in the world to come.

We know that many wonderful elements of greatness will enter into the making of the future life of bliss. But of none of those elements are our theologians so sure as they are of that glorious thing, knowledge. Practically they study eternal life from the point of view of knowledge only. It may be called the one hard, indubitable and palpable fact of eternal life most clearly known to us. We are no longer among symbols, but we are dealing with things we might almost call concrete when we are treating of the knowledge of the blessed in heaven; all symbolism resolves itself into this reality, knowledge, in our doctrine on the future life, and it is this intellectualism of our eternal hope that saves Catholic theology from floundering about aimlessly in mere sentimentality.

Let us take one instance only of the solidifying of all symbolism into hard concepts through this element of knowledge. There is nothing more common than the desire of being one day amongst the angels, of sharing the life of the angels. He must be a hopeless materialist, and a greater sinner to boot, who looks not grave when he is told that his predeceased mother or wife is among the angels. Here, then, we have a magical expression, something that gives a ray of transient idealism to the dullest country yokel. Very few men in England would take such sayings to be meaningless. Yet what can such expressions mean? Far be it from me to call them pious

platitudes; they are precious remnants of an idealism that was once strong
in our people. How, then, are our dead friends amongst the angels? How
do they become angels? I know most people are in need of such explana-
tions. For them to be amongst the angels is the summary of all bliss, and
the cessation of all such imperfections as made the beloved person, when
still in flesh and blood, something less ideal. Yet it is the theologian's office
to be ready to give the reality that lies behind symbolism; for, after all, to
be with the angels is merely a figure of speech. We cannot be amongst the
heavenly spirits in the way we move about in our well-furnished rooms.
Nor are we placed amongst the angels as we find ourselves mixed up in a
human crowd, elbowing each other, making space the narrower the more
numerous we are.

Theology, therefore, makes an appeal to our intellect, and asks us to
think of this matter in terms of knowledge. We shall be, through God's
grace, amongst the angels of God; we shall be like the heavenly spirits,
because in all things our intellectual life will resemble the intellectual life
of those glorious beings. The least of us will be a mighty people in himself,
as his mind will have an enlargement so wonderful that all things that
are not God Himself will be below, not above such a mind. The of God's
natural creation, with all its immensities, will be held by the minds of the
elect in heaven, as a ripe fruit is held in the hand of the man who gathers
it. God alone, and the supernatural order which is God's life in the elect,
will be above the minds of the elect, will be a thing to look up to, not to
look down upon. In the world to come man will truly be where his mind
is, and if his mind be found capable of emulating in all things the angelic
mind, man in very deed will be as one who goes in and out among the
angelic choirs.

V

THE WORLD OF LOVE

PEOPLE DIFFER GREATLY in the nature of their mental perplexities about the future life. For all of us the blessed existence which is the matter of our hope has puzzles and mysteries. We know instinctively that the perfect life which will be the portion of the elect must be a radical solution of all our practical problems; but this instinctive anticipation of a happy ending to the most involved situations does not bring with itself the answer as to how the problem will be solved.

Thus a patient and tolerant reader of these articles, a Doctor of Divinity to boot, told me quite candidly that the only problem concerning future life that could truly vex a thoughtful mind is the reconciliation, in heaven, of the apparently incompatible temperaments of human beings, and he hinted that all my labors will be in vain as long as I offer no solution of this theological poser, how men who dislike each other so cordially here on earth may be found one day blissfully united in the common joy of heaven.

My friend's worries set me thinking, and I find, as one sometimes does in life, that I have been living on the very edge of an immense mystery without being aware of it.

Yes, human beings do differ, they do dislike each other, they are separated by impassable antipathies; is it not one of the best things in life to be away from one's fellow-men? Yet if heaven is anything, it is an eternal fondness for each other amongst all the elect. How, then, is this great change, this astonishing fusion of so many conflicting elements into one pure mass of gold, to come about? I speak here of antipathies and dissimilarities of temperament, not of hatred and enmity. A man who hates his fellow-man, a man who is truly an enemy to another man, is an easy theological case: We know what to make of him, his fate in eternity does not puzzle us. If he die in his hatred, if his soul depart this life in a state of enmity, we have no further concern about him:

> Whosoever hateth his brother is a murderer. And you know that no
> murderer hath eternal life abiding in himself (1 JOHN 3:15).

If there be two men hating each other, and they die in their hatred, we need not make a spiritual problem of this and ask ourselves how in God's name two such men could ever sit together at the eternal banquet of Christ. They will never sit together in the kingdom of heaven; they will hate each other as long as their dark souls have any sort of personal existence.

Some of my readers may be inclined to find this solution of one portion of our problem rather too drastic. If there be two men who cannot love each other whilst they journey onwards on the road of life, they will never love each other; and this mutual hatred, if it be true hatred, will be a gulf between them for all the aeons of eternity, unless there be repentance before the goal of death be reached. It is perhaps a startling thought for some of us; but after all, if heaven is not the home of charity, what is it?

Not many years ago I happened to be a neutral witness of a very animated dispute between some rather eminent men with a pronounced tinge of that traitorous form of uncharitableness called *esprit de corps*. Will my readers believe me if I tell them that the men were members of two rival religious orders? As the dispute waxed fiercer and fiercer, I could not resist the temptation to whisper to a friend, also a neutral in the dispute, that

I saw no way out of the spiritual *impasse* except an act of God, by which He would assign different portions of His beautiful Paradise to the different good men of rival religious garbs. I-had in my mind the text about the many mansions. But my friend was of a less naïve mind. "Different heavens!" he ejaculated, "I should think that none of them will go to any heaven anywhere if they carry on as they do."

My companion's grim exclamation set me meditating. With hatreds, then, I am not concerned here: heaven does not heal hatreds, but heaven heals dislikes. Such, at any rate, is our hope. We may love, and yet dislike; we love in the true Gospel sense, wishing our fellow-man every blessing, temporal and spiritual, but this does not mean that we like him, that we find it easy to like him. Is it not the peculiar power and grace of Christian charity to make us love people whom we find it difficult to like? Now we feel instinctively that in heaven there can be no such duality, no such division of feeling and sentiment. We want a Paradise where we can like everybody, and where everybody is expected to like us.

How, then, will this be done? Certainly at no point in our investigations on the life of the world to come are we in greater need of one of those pregnant phrases of St. Paul which give at the same time the problem and the solution:

> Now this I say, brethren, that flesh and blood cannot possess the kingdom of God: neither shall corruption possess incorruption (1 COR 15:50).

This we feel instinctively. It is our difficulty all along. We are convinced that if our friends were left as they are, with all those traits of an unamiable character that come from flesh and blood, they had better remain outside heaven. No doubt they may be saying the same of us. Now for the solution:

> In a moment, in the twinkling of an eye, at the last trumpet: for the trumpet shall sound and the dead shall rise again incorruptible. And we shall be changed (1 COR 15:52).

We shall be changed; what more could we wish for? It is our daily wish and prayer in the trials of human intercourse; we wish nothing more than that people should be changed; and very seldom does anyone formulate in his heart any darker wish about us than that we should be changed. We shall be, all of us, changed beings; and this blessed change will be the reward of the elect for all their patience and all their forbearance with the infirmities, shortcomings, and antipathies of others.

Perhaps some of my readers will stop here and follow me no farther, being completely absorbed by mental speculations as to the nature of the change required to make a given person lovable whom the Gospel bids us to love. This could prove a most pleasant reverie, and perhaps quite harmless. Anyhow, if anyone is thus engaged in visualizing the future, I escape being asked a difficult philosophical question which must inevitably crop up at this point: how this change is to be reconciled with another most precise truth, the preservation of our personal identity in the future life, a point I have carefully elaborated.

Our theology of eternal life is based on the assumption that in the world to come we shall be the same people we were on earth. Without this identity there is simply no eternal life for any of us. So we are driven to the conclusion that our happy future state implies both a sameness and a change; we shall be the same People, yet we shall be changed people. There will be something in us that will link our immortal being with our mortal career, that career in which many of us were the object of Christian love, without on that account being very much liked; and there will be in us something quite new, so as to make us entirely lovable to every other one of God's elect in His wide world of final sanctity.

No doubt it will seem to many an observer of his fellow-creatures that certain unattractive characteristics appear to be of the very essence of the person: it would be as impossible to think of him or her without those idiosyncrasies as to think of a tree without branches and leaves. I fully admit that this transformation of man inside the very narrow compass of his personal identity makes an appeal to all our faith in the power of God's grace. But is it not the very thing that makes Christianity the marvel it is, that it should have the power to change man so completely without destroying in him his personal identity? Christianity has no love for theories of Eastern origin about man's virtual absorption in a vaster scheme, in a purer whole; Christianity wants strong, energetic, powerfully characterized individuals, without any vapors of ill-defined existences about them. Let a man be in himself an all-absorbing center of life and influence; Christianity promises not to change him into something vague, something impersonal, but into a most lovable giant of strength and will.

But how will this be done? How will the strong ones become as amiable as guileless babes? In which portion of man's nature will that change promised by St. Paul take place? The obvious thing would be to say that the change will take place in the heart; our heart will be changed, and we shall find ourselves liking each other most cordially. Yet this is the very portion of man's nature that I have to omit in this investigation as to the nature of the blessed change in man and woman. For throughout I am supposing that the heart is all right; I am supposing the existence of true charity, of that degree of love without which there is no salvation whatever. The moment that the heart gives way to likes and dislikes, you have more than an incompatibility of temperament, you have hatred, and I have made it clear, I hope, that I owe no explanation as to the future state of any man who dies with hatred in his heart.

The heart must be good and loving always. This we take for granted; all Christians must be united in their hearts if they expect to enter into the glorious kingdom. But, with the exception of this central portion of our being, even we Christians, who have the firstfruits of the Spirit, may be greatly at variance in most other things that make a human life. Our minds, our thinking powers, go in opposite directions. I am not, of course, speaking here of the truths of the Catholic faith; the unanimous acceptance of those truths among us is a part of the unity of heart I am speaking of, as no man believes who has not the good will to do so.

Now it is this diversity of mind which is, to my thinking, the chief source of our being so little in sympathy with each other. We see things so differently; we take such opposite views of the same events; we judge with finality in directions that are diametrically opposed to each other. All this we do because we know no better. Now it will be the first result of entering into the blessed vision of God that we shall see all things in the light of God; there will be no possibility of our not seeing all things in the same way because we shall be gazing at infinite Truth. Misunderstanding and misrepresentation will be impossible, nor will there be the small mind that is in constant dread of being made the plaything of the more powerful understanding. I think that, when all is said, narrowness of mind is the one defect which is the root of all our dissimilarities of character, which prevents our mixing well and blending into one organic whole with an untrammeled flow of vitality.

Now this narrowness is excluded from eternal life by the very laws of that life. The great change that will come over man is thus expressed by our Lord Himself:

> But they that shall be accounted worthy of that world and of the resurrection from the dead shall neither be married nor take wives. Neither can they die any more: for we are equal to the angels and are the children of God, being the children of the resurrection (LUKE 22:35-36).

The elect are so different in their qualities from what they were here on earth, simply because they are the equals of the angels. In my last article I tried to make it clear how this equality with the angels must mean, above all things, equality in intellectual vision. Through this great vision, through this perfect expansion human mind, we shall be the "children of God, being the children of the resurrection." By all the laws of nature and grace, beings thus elevated, thus enlarged, thus spiritualized, must be lovable beyond our mortal comprehension.

Our Lord insinuates in the wonderful utterance just quoted that there is an intimate connection between the mystery of our happy resurrection and our adoptive, divine sonship. The elect in heaven will the "children of God, being the children of the resurrection." The glorious resurrection will make those that are saved into children of God, into the equals of the angels. The resurrection itself will be a great change for man's nature.

Perhaps some of my readers will think a fullness of knowledge an insufficient explanation of that total transformation of our rather difficult human temperaments and characters. Is there not in our very constitution, in our whole temperament, nay, even in our bodily system, in our nerves and sinews, something that is not compatible with other natures? Perhaps the very much used expression of "getting on each other's nerves" may be taken literally in its physiological sense as a description of the thorny path on which divine charity has to walk here on earth. A mere knowing of everything, a mere understanding of ourselves, of other people and things, need not bring about by itself that peace and concord, that lovableness, without which we could not think of heaven. Is there not a bodily element in human antipathy, besides a mental defect?

On the whole I am quite willing to make the bodily portion of our nature to be the partial cause, at least, of our dissonances of temperament. The instinctive hostilities which we find in the animal kingdom between various kinds of beasts come naturally to one's mind when one looks at the unreasoning dislike between classes of men. But it is hardly a subject which would add to the edification these articles are meant to give to the pious. In any case, however deep-rooted our antipathies may be, seated as they are in our very blood, transmitted from generation to generation, why despair? The resurrection will make us into new beings, with no other heredity than that of Christ and His blessed Mother, with new blood into which the Blood of the Son of God has entered as a divine element through the influence of the eucharistic mystery:

Now this I say, brethren, that flesh and blood cannot possess the kingdom of God (1 Cor 15:50).

So much of that which is "in our blood" is the subconscious origin of our animosities, articulate and inarticulate. None of it will be found in man in the resurrection. St. Paul is emphatic to the verge of being brutal when he tackles the general question of the renewal of our sense life in Christ through the resurrection:

> Meat for the belly and the belly for the meats: but God shall destroy both it and them. ... Now God hath raised up the Lord and will raise us up also by his power. Know you not that Your bodies are the members of Christ (1 COR 6:13-14)?

Nothing short of another such destruction will ever be able to eradicate from that very elusive portion of ourselves, "our blood," the seeds of animosities as ancient as history. Their destruction will be as radical as the destruction of the meats and their organs. Instead, there will be a new creature,

> according to the image of him that created him. Where there is neither Gentile nor Jew, circumcision nor uncircumcision, Barbarian nor Scythian, bond nor free. But Christ is all and in all (COL 3:11).

The human conditions here enumerated by St. Paul are as far apart as could possibly exist between beings of the same species. If such diversities can be healed in the glory of the risen Christ, we need not despair to find a solution of the very practical difficulty how two men belonging to two warring nations may still find themselves blissfully united in the world to come, though they passed out of this world in a death struggle in which each one believed himself to be in the right. There will be only one race of human beings in the world to come, the race that will spring up in the hour of the great rebirth, " in the regeneration when the Son of man shall sit on the seat of his majesty" (MATT 19 28).

VI

CHRIST THE BUILDER OF ETERNITY

W HEN WE HEAR the Son of God declaring in His Gospel that He
will build up His Church on the Rock, we are in presence of
one of those pregnant utterances on which human imagination may feed
forever without there being any danger of distorting into something ex-
travagant the simplicity of the primitive concept. Christ declares that He is
a builder; that He is determined to erect an edifice on a foundation strong
enough for any superstructure. Where need we stop with such an idea to
start from? The Architect has infinite genius, infinite power, infinite resourcefulness. His foundation is chosen with infinite care, and the life of
the great Builder is eternity itself. No human imagination is capable of
exhausting the meaning of Christ's words when He says that He will build
His Church on the Rock. "The city of the living God, the heavenly Jerusalem" (HEB 12:22) are classical expressions to represent the glorious world to
come; the size and the beauty of the heavenly city need not have any other
limits than the limits set to the resources of the Builder. Now we have said
that the Builder does all things, not with finiteness, but in infinitude.

There is one feature in this immense labour of the Son of God which
may become to us the source of great mental peace, if it be properly envis-

aged. It is in keeping with all the doctrinal canons of orthodoxy in the matter of divine grace and predestination to hold that the plan of the heavenly Jerusalem is a thing fixed from the very beginning, with no casual alterations or additions as time goes on. In other words, mankind here on earth is merely the quarry from which are taken materials for the city of the living God. When the city is completed, mankind will lose all its justification for a further prolongation of its existence here. Mankind living on this planet is as entirely subservient to the needs of the divine Builder who has resolved to build the heavenly Jerusalem as the quarry is entirely subservient to the needs of the edifice that is being erected miles away. When once the edifice is completed the quarry is closed down.

To put it less symbolically and more theologically: the number of the elect who will constitute the eternal city of the living God is a quantity which is fixed in God's mind from all eternity, and when once that number is reached, God loses interest in the history of the human race as it is worked out here on earth. Moreover, the degree of created sanctity to be reached by man and angel is a fixed measure, and the hour in which the limit will be reached will be truly the consummation of the mystery of God.

This view of God's activity ought to be most gratifying to our minds, as it is the Christian answer to one of the most persistent difficulties that beset our path, the apparent casualness with which the just are taken away from the midst of their labor and their enterprises. Is it not a temptation to our faith in the wisdom of things to see how the useless members of mankind seem endowed with a most disconcerting vitality and longevity, whilst God's workers are snatched away before they have had time to put their best foot forward? There seems so little plan, so little design in the manner in which the trees of human life are felled by the axe of death. But if we habitually think in terms of divine architecture, if we remember that there is a plan of wonderful completeness and perfection lying on the table of Christ in the kingdom of His Father, then we shall wonder no longer why the just man is taken away with such scant consideration for the needs of other men in this world, and why the man of mercy is snatched away in the very act of giving, though there be still so many empty hands stretched out towards him. The determining factors are to be looked for, not in the needs of man here on earth, but in the needs of the heavenly Jerusalem, and in the requirements of the great enterprise which the Son of God has in hand.

It means, of course, a very great reversal of values; it means that the earthly history of man is a thing without a plan, without a design, mankind being merely subservient to the necessities of the "building of God." But has any man ever been able to detect a design in the so-called historical developments of the human race, except a theorizing monomaniac? Mankind's history is at best made up of big chunks of events; it is not the working out of a plan. It has the features of a busy stone quarry with blasted rocks of various sizes; it certainly possesses none of the symmetry of a construction.

Theories about continuousness of evolution in mankind are the most compromising occupation of the human intellect. You have hardly uttered your generalization when some fact of a contrary nature pricks your logical mind like a needle. Of course there is a plan, a superb plan, but it is not to be found on this earth; it has the Son of God in heaven pondering over it; it has principalities and spiritualities in divine places scanning it; it is to be found at the gates of the still unfinished heavenly Jerusalem.

All that happens to the children of men is the result of exact calculation in the higher spheres of intellectual life. One of the seven angels that were seen by St John pouring out on guilty mankind the vials full of the seven last plagues appears the moment after in a very different role; he is no longer a destroyer, but a constructor; a clear indication that all destructions ordered by God are mere quarrying of His building materials. He stands before the eyes of John with the builder's rule in his hand:

And he that spoke with me had a measure of a reed of gold, to measure the city and the gate thereof and the wall (REV 21:15).

The burden of this my apocalyptic song today is a trill of joy at the thought that each Christian life is meant to be a masterpiece, something that is perfectly fitted for God's great construction. Our world to come is not a vague Hades, peopled with flitting shades, however white and contented. It is not a mere crowd of blessed beings sanctified in Christ. Our world to come is essentially a thing of hierarchy, where each blessed one fills a great role, has his proper niche of splendor; and the whole labour of sanctification is to shape us all for the very place in the divine edifice which is meant to be ours from all eternity.

> Many a blow and biting sculpture
>   Polished well those stones elect,
> In their places now compacted
>   By the heavenly Architect,
> Who therewith hath willed for ever
>   That his Palace should be decked.

Like all heavenly truths, this truth is balm both to the strong and the weak. The strong man in God who labors with success cannot help being startled at the mere suggestion that within an hour death may bring low himself and his schemes. But what are his schemes by the side of Christ's great scheme? He can never pretend to be more than a stone that is being prepared for the "holy city Jerusalem coming down out of heaven from God" (REV 21:10), even if he were Peter himself, or Peter's successor, on whom Christ builds the Church as on a solid rock. The weak, the apparently useless Christian will find in this hierarchic visualizing of the world to come the remedy for one very constant affliction of most good souls in humble conditions, the depressing conviction of their uselessness to God. How could anyone be useless whom the Holy Ghost prepares for a particular place in the Temple of God? Having the measure of a mere man, when taken up by the divine Builder he all at once has the measure of an angel, as his chosen and predestined position in the holy walls imparts to his individual personality the style of the whole structure.

And he (the angel) measured the wall thereof, an hundred forty-four cubits, the measure of a man, which is of an angel (Rev 21:17).

The heavenly Jerusalem is evidently meant to be a great surprise, something got ready behind a screen and shown forth on its day in its final glory. The completed city is not said to ascend from earth to heaven, but, on the contrary, it comes down from heaven, where it had been in course of construction as behind a screen during the centuries of Christ's activities.

And he took me up in spirit to a great and high mountain: and he showed me the holy city Jerusalem, coming down out of heaven from God, having the glory of God. And the light thereof was like to a precious stone, as to the jasper stone, even as crystal, and it had a wall great and high, having twelve gates (Rev 21:10).

It is the work of the divine Builder, the effort of centuries. But who can so well afford to have long duration schemes as the One to whom a thousand years are as one day and one day as a thousand years?

It is still the kindliest philosophy about the destinies of the human race to consider humanity as the rough materials from which are hewn the stones of the heavenly Jerusalem. The untold millions of human beings that have dwelt or are dwelling on this globe of ours are not something disproportionate, something bewildering to the mind of the Christian thinker who has imagination enough to see the full bearing of the divinely inspired expressions that represent the society of the happy world to come as a building of God. The size of that divine construction is such, from the very character of the Builder, as to make countless generations of human beings here on earth appear no larger than, say, a hill-top from which are taken the stones of some magnificent medieval minster. Let us think first of the city of the living God in heaven, and our minds will be more ready to range humanity and to give it its proper values.

A few summers ago I had a visit from two excellent Catholic thinkers and writers on matters of the spiritual world. Sitting under a tree in the

Abbey grounds we came upon this very point, in our exchange of views, the baffling multiplicity of the descendants of Adam, each of them having an immortal soul to save. We had little to say to each other on the subject, and we looked grave like men who have seen a ghost. "It is a tremendous mystery," one of us muttered, and we sat in silence for some time, like the friends of Job. We might, of course, have remembered our Psalms and quoted a most appropriate text: "The wicked walk round about: according to thy highness, thou hast multiplied the children of men" (Ps 11:9). But our best consolation should have been the Apocalypse, as it is for all Catholic thinkers who are deeply impressed by the fatalities that dog the footsteps of mankind.

When St. John was given the vision of the holy city of Jerusalem coming down out of heaven from God, he had first to be taken up in spirit to a very lofty summit, so as to expand his range of vision:

> And there came one of the seven angels ... and he took me up in spirit to a great and high mountain: and he showed me the holy city Jerusalem, coming down out of heaven from God (REV 21:9).

My friends sat in sadness on that afternoon because no such elevation of spirit had ever been granted them. Were it but vouchsafed to us to behold the eternal city of God as it were from a high mountain, then we should see at a glance why the human race must be infinitely numerous, according to our standard of calculation, in order to furnish to God the living stones for His high edifice. In very truth, according to His highness, He has multiplied the children of men.

VII

The Phenomenon of Death

I<small>T IS IMPOSSIBLE</small> to go any distance in our pious speculations on the life of the world to come without feeling the need of a guiding voice to tell us how much of it will be the survival or, at any rate, the continuance of the present world, with its manifold lives and existences.

We are carried away by the beauty of the distant scenery, by the scintillating splendor of the snow-capped Alps which we descry from afar. Our eyes have a wonderful way of creating the illusion that they are the whole body, as vision seems to render the functions of all the other members of the body superfluous and unreal. But this is a gratuitous and unfair assumption on the part of our organs of sight. In the most exhilarating feast of the eyes, as when they are gazing on the glories of distant scenery, there is the subconscious certainty in man that it is in his power to move towards that far-off object. Truly the whole body contributes to the feast of the eyes, because the whole body is bent forward in an effort to reach the fascinating mountain top.

In our greatest raptures for the future and far-away splendors there is the voice within us that says that we ourselves, in our own flesh, shall be there sooner or later; that our own feet will carry us thither. So, by the side of the article in the Creed that is like a vision of the glories of the world to come, there is another article of belief, which, like a trusted fellow-traveler, never ceases to remind the eyes which have the vision that the object of the vision is to be possessed and taken hold of by the whole body of man. Our belief in the resurrection of the flesh is more than a completion of our belief in the life of the world to come, it is as integral a part of it as my locomotive powers are an integral part of my delight in beautiful scenery; it is given to me not only to see, but also to ascend the mountain in my own strength of body. Our faith in the resurrection of the flesh is our faith in God's power to preserve intact human individuality through the countless aeons of eternity, or, to put it less learnedly, it is our faith in God's power to give eternal life to the very people who journey now on the dusty road of temporal life.

If Christ had met St. Paul on the Appian Way as the Apostle was making for Rome, if He had touched the careworn traveler on the forehead, and if in the life-giving energy of that touch the Son of God had transformed the body of Paul's lowliness into a glorified body, to the image of Christ's own body, it would have been a very evident instance of the power of Jesus to give eternal life to the very man who a moment before was groaning under the burden of a mortal life. When we profess our faith in the resurrection of the flesh we profess this very thing, in a broad way of speaking, that Christ has the power to transform all our temporal lives into eternal lives, so that the glories of the World to come will be reached in very truth by the same individual who saw them and saluted them from afar off, not by some new being of a different origin. The two beliefs in the resurrection of the flesh and in the life of the world to come are inseparable companions. If one remained behind the other would be sure to go astray. An eternal life that was no resurrection of the flesh would be like a pair of eyes detached from the body.

Someone will say that my hypothetical meeting of Christ with St. Paul on the Appian Way is no fair parable for so great a truth, as no man ever passes from mortality into eternal life in so sudden a way. Do we not, all of us, vanish from the surface of the earth without ever feeling that magical and potent touch of Christ? How, then, can it be said with truth that our mortal puts on immortality? How can it be said with truth that the way-farer is the identical individual who later on reaches the mountain top?

Now this is one of those subtle occasions when Christian thought is at its best, because it is on the scent of a great truth; for all great truths have their subtle scents. So Christian thought is all for contending that it really does not matter in the least whether a man be met by Christ on the Appian Way, or whether a man lie for two thousand years as indistinguishable dust in the catacombs hard by on the same road. In both cases it will be equally true to say that the good servant, after toiling for the Master, is bidden to enter into the joy of his Lord, in the body in which he has served, with the members that have been busy all day long in the household services of the great King. Christian thought admits no real, no radical interruption or difference in my two assumptions: the case of him who is transformed from mortality into glory, or of that other who enters glory from repose of a thousand years in the grave; in both instances the identity of person is equally complete.

We do not, of course, deny the physical fact of death; we are not so silly as to pretend that death is mere illusion. But we have our views on God's power of restoring that human personality which is so badly damaged by death. This restoring power of God is indeed a most important part of our theories on the nature of God, and unless we give that power unlimited scope one-half of Christianity becomes meaningless to us. In whichever way a creature has come to grief, whatever be the extent of that creature's ruin-ation, even were it positively annihilated, it is in God's power to restore it to its pristine existence, to its former life, with such completeness that the most piercing eye of man or angel could not detect a flaw in the restored creature. It matters little for the moment whether in such restoration God makes use of the scattered fragments of the former existence: He may do so or may not do so. His universal power to recreate what has ceased to exist is a truth by itself, and is of unlimited application. In the raising up of the dead God will make use of the separated and scattered elements of the previous personality. There is much to be said on this bringing together of the disjointed parts of our human individualities on the day that Christ will destroy death and all its works. But before coming to that more specific article Of Christian doctrine may we not delight in the unlimited spaces of God's activities and powers, and find pleasure in the thought that the restoring omnipotence of God will have wonderful surprises in store for all His creatures?

Without entering yet into the individual features of the resurrection at the end of the world, we can prepare the ground for further thought by a study of that higher aspect of God's character which is expressed so well by St. Paul when he says of God that He "calleth those things that are not, as those that are" (ROM 4:17). For a thing to hear the call of God it is not necessary that it should actually exist: the call itself will make it exist the moment it is wanted. If the thing has ceased to exist, this cessation is nothing to God; His calling for it will give it existence again; and its period of nonexistence, its interruption of activities, of life, of thought, of personal consciousness, will be no more than a sweet moment of sound sleep. There is simply no limit to that power of God to make the past live again. We do not know to what extent God will make use of that power of His. The Christian belief in the general judgment at the end of the world's history implies a raising up of the past on a scale nearly infinite. It will be a reconstruction of the dead past which will rank in splendor of divine achievement with the resurrection of dead humanity.

Let us take it for granted that all things, with all their lights and shades, can be made to exist again through God's power. Whether the created thing has been annihilated, whether it has been broken up into fragments, whether it has simply ceased to exist, matters little to God's power: He merely bids it stand before him again as it was of yore. "For he (God) is not the God of the dead, but of the living: for all live to him" (LUKE 20:38). There is no death in the sight of God, as it is a matter of supreme indifference to divine omnipotence whether a man have the breath of life in his nostrils or not; if God wants to speak to him, he will be there before God, who "calleth those things that are not, as those that are." To bring back the past has always been one of man's dreams. In this, as in many other unspoken aspirations, we prove our faint and distant resemblance to our Maker, who can do all these things in a truly royal manner.

But to revert to our entry into the glorious world to come. Our Scriptures have a wonderful way of overlooking the incident of death. They couple man's actual life and man's eternal life in heaven with such supreme ease that one might be tempted to think that they expect every generation of men to walk bodily into the next world, there to receive their due, as the hired laborer walks home in the evening with his pay in his hand. If our inspired writings admit of a break in man's life-career, the break is merely a falling asleep for awhile. But for all practical purposes the Scriptures consider man's progress as an uninterrupted march from this world into the next, soul and body. It is because our God is a God, not of the dead but of the living, "for all live to him." In the infinite resourcefulness of His restoring omnipotence, the man that has been in a grave for ten thousand years is as completely brought back to his personal consciousness as if he had nodded in a light slumber whilst riding a horse.

We ought to look upon this disregard for the incident of death as one of the characteristics of the New Testament, a characteristic not to be found in any other religious system. It matters so very little, in New Testament thought, when the Master comes for the great reckoning, be it "at even, or at midnight, or at the cock-crowing, or in the morning" (MARK 13:35). At whatever time of the world's history He chooses to step on the scenes, all men will be to Him, not as past or present, but as watchers or revelers. Truly they will come to Him not in their death, but in their life, as "all live to him." Unless we have before our eyes this power of God to restore all things as they were, much of the New Testament language will appear to us to be an unwarrantable boldness. But with this enlightened view of God's true character every generation of Christians can say of itself that it is waiting for the coming of Christ in the clouds. The period of the bodily death is merely the sleep of the ten virgins in the heavy hours that precede midnight, as they await the bridegroom.

To the men who hate Him, Christ speaks of His great coming in the clouds as if it were to be witnessed by them in their lifetime. Annas and

Caiphas, and the whole tribe of mercenary pontiffs with their satellites and parasites will all be there, on that great day, to contemplate with their own eyes the astonishing reversal of roles:

> Again the high priest asked him: Art thou the Christ, the Son of the blessed God? And Jesus said to him: I am. And you shall see the Son of man sitting on the right hand of the power of God and coming with the clouds of heaven (Mark 4:61-62).

Let us note the strength of that phrase "you shall see." The group of embittered men who dart such glances of hatred at Him now will have that surprise one day. They will die at their appointed time, a few years after Christ's ascension. But this in no wise interferes with the continuousness of the drama. Some of the actors will leave the scenes for a while, but they will all be there for the final act.

It may be said that the dominant idea of the New Testament is this restoration of all things, this rebirth of mankind, this "regeneration," as the evangelist puts it. Christ wants the whole of mankind, to deal with it as a shepherd deals with his flock:

> And all nations shall be gathered together before him: and he shall separate them one from another, as the shepherd separateth the sheep from the goats (Matt 25:32).

The raising up of the dead is merely a means towards that great end: the cancellation of the marks of death on human history. The bodily resurrection is not even the complete compass of God's power in that respect. The restoration means more than the bringing back of human bodies: it implies the reconstruction of the whole past of the human race:

> For there is nothing covered that shall not be revealed: nor hidden that shall not be known (Luke 12:2).

No power has ever been so futile as the power of death. It looks as if it were an interruption of all things, and yet there is not a whisper of love or hatred which it has been able truly to imprison:

> For whatsoever things you have spoken in darkness shall be pub-
> lished in the light: and that which you have spoken in the ear in the
> chambers shall be preached on the housetops (LUKE 12:3).

Death plays an exceedingly small role in New Testament thought. It
certainly stops nothing, and offers no hindrance to the full and harmoni-
ous working out of the divine plan. God's restoring power bulks so large
in the Gospel that death, by the side of it, seems to be a grotesque menial.
This restoring power is the amazing thing: the powers of death melt away
before it like a wraith at sunrise:

> Wonder not at this: for the hour cometh, wherein all that are in the
> graves shall hear the voice of the Son of God. And they that have
> done good things shall come forth unto the resurrection of life: but
> they that have done evil, unto the resurrection of judgement (JOHN
> 5:28-29).

Do we not admire the man who loves his work as if he were to live
forever, and who lives as if he were to die soon? Perseverance in his un-
dertakings for God's glory, and purity of soul, are happily welded together
in such a man. As for the Son of God, moving among men in the days of
His mortality, I shall in future think of Him as loving His work not only
as one who is to live forever, but also as one who knows that His work will
endure for ever, that none of those that are His ever sink below the horizon
of which He is the center:

> That which my Father has given me is greater than all: and no one
> can snatch them out of the hand of my Father (1 JOHN 10:29).

VIII

CHRIST THE FIRSTFRUITS
OF THEM THAT SLEEP

OF ALL THE BRILLIANT METAPHORS which enshrine Christian thought, no one comes nearer to taking the palm than that expression of St. Paul by which he describes Christ as the firstfruits of them that sleep:

> But now Christ is risen from the dead, the firstfruits of them that sleep. ... But everyone in his own order: the firstfruits, Christ: then they that are of Christ, who have believed in his Coming (1 COR 15:20, 23).

The sleepers are the dead: they are the seed hidden in the ground. The whole world is a field teeming with the hidden activities of that seed. The winter that keeps the field frost-bound may be ever so long, but the unseen palpitations of life inside the sleeping seed become more vigorous as the winter advances. A long winter never discourages the faith of the husband-man in Nature's truthfulness; he is more afraid of Nature's momentary angers when, in the glory of summer, the heat, that seems life itself, contains the mortal shower of hailstones. A protracted winter, on the contrary, is no trial to the legitimate hopes of the one who has ploughed and sown his field. That the final triumph of the divine life should be preceded by a very long winter sleep ought not to give scandal to our Christian minds. If we are wise in the things of God's world we shall think more of the quality of the grain that has been entrusted to the land in autumn than of the grim way winter has of appearing endless and unchangeable.

St. Paul's metaphor completes and emulates in sheer force of expressiveness the older metaphor that comes from the lips of the divine Poet, Christ:

> The hour is come that the Son of man should be glorified. Amen, amen, I say to you, unless the grain of wheat falling into the ground die, itself remaineth alone. But if it die, it bringeth forth much fruit (JOHN 12:23-25).

Christ Himself is a grain of wheat in the grasp of the winter. Winter therefore cannot be an evil thing if it holds such a trust. It may be long; it is not an evil power, but a good power.

Piecing together the two halves of the same sketch, one from the hand of Christ, the other from the hand of Christ's Apostle, we can easily find out how we ourselves are in the picture. Christ is a grain of wheat reposing in the frost-bound field; but Christ is also the firstfruits from the great field of them that sleep in death. Now it is in the very nature of firstfruits to be of the same quality as the rest of the harvest. Therefore we must conclude that the other sleepers are wonderful grain too; we need not be uneasy about the final result; one and the same winter embosoms all the sleepers, Christ and His elect.

The firstfruits of any crop are not necessarily precocious fruits. In fact, is it not this very circumstance that makes firstfruits to be such a blessing, that they are a good augury for the whole crop? The firstfruits must be culled from the main growth; firstfruits are essentially representative; they are the voice of the ripening field, and speak to God and man the joyous message of the year's fertility. If it were in the nature of firstfruits to be exceptional in growth, to be precocious productions of the soil, they could be no longer the sacramental thing they are in the older ritual ordinances, as their life would be something apart from the life that has sprung from under the winter's covering of snow. An ear that reaches maturity weeks before the normal harvesting moon, just because it grows up in a nook of privileged sunshine, could never be offered up on the altar as the firstfruits to God, for it would contain no reliable message of the true hopes of the husbandman. You can always grow grapes in a sheltered spot, under the care of the solicitous gardener who nurses a vine as if it were his own child. The juicy grape will be welcome at the rich man's table, but it will have no voice to tell us how the great vineyards of the world's sunny climes have fared in the year, how the heavenly Father has blessed this wide earth of ours. Firstfruits must share the conditions under which the whole harvest approaches maturity. There must be perfect community between the sheaf that is brought to God's altar as the firstfruits and the sheaves that are carried into man's granary.

Does my reader begin to perceive what a beautiful and consoling thing St. Paul said when he called Christ the firstfruits of them that sleep? Christ's resurrection is not an exotic thing transplanted from the hot regions of heaven to our cold earth. It is not a flower that peeps out on a barren landscape from a sheltered fold in the warm red rocks which catch all the sun there is, as daffodils will behave sometimes in Devon in the first weeks of the new year. Much less is Christ's resurrection like the carefully nurtured grape under the heated roof of the wealthy man's conservatory. Christ's resurrection belongs to the great, open, windswept fields where the other dead are sown, furrow after furrow. That all the dead should rise again is a thing that need not make us marvel more than that the Son of God should rise from His grave, the moment we are assured that He is the firstfruits of all of us who go down into our graves.

In the things of God, and, for the matter of that, in the things of the angels of God, time is the one element that does not matter; God is supremely indifferent to time. It is to Him what the dust of the road is to us, a thing that has nothing to do with our march, either backwards or forwards:

> But of this one thing be not ignorant, my beloved, that one day
> with the Lord is as a thousand years, and a thousand years as one
> day (2 PET 3:8).

St. Peter is evidently anxious that we should learn well by rote this truth of
God's supreme indifference to time. Time is long only to those who carry
burdens; if in the absorption of some great happiness you have ceased to
advert to the things that surround you, time for that period of your life has
ceased to be anything to you. In all exactness, no man waits for the day
of the great resurrection longer than the short number of the years of his
mortal life. The blessed soul of St. Paul, to quote a personal example, in
the unchanging vision of God's glory, could not be said to spend its time in
waiting for the resurrection. In the bliss of God's vision time is truly abol-
ished for the soul of the saved in heaven. Christ, the firstfruits of them that
sleep, rises from the dead before us, it is true; but from God's angle, from
the angle of the happy spirits, this priority is more truly a priority of order
than a priority of time. What is time outside our solar astronomy?

> And as in Adam all die, so also in Christ all shall be made alive. But
> everyone in his own order: the firstfruits, Christ: then they that are
> of Christ, who have believed in his coming 1 Cor 15:22-23).

In our thoughts on the great mystery of the resurrection it is of supreme
importance never to isolate Christ's rising from the dead from the resurrection of all flesh at the end of that great tragedy, the history of the human race.
If once we begin to take to heart St. Peter's injunctions not to consider astro-
nomical time as a factor in the things of God, it will become more apparent
to us that Christ's resurrection and our resurrection at the end of the world
are truly one and the same spiritual phenomenon. The intervening delay is
merely the patience of One who plays a long and deep game:

> The Lord delayeth not his promise, as some imagine, but dealeth
> patiently for your sake, not willing that any should perish, but that
> all should return to penance (3 PET 3:9).

The Player never sleeps, the game is never interrupted, and the final move will show how much He is Master of the situation. To the watchful observer it will seem as if there were no more reason for the game to come to an end at that moment than at any other moment, either before or after. Yet with one last master-stroke the climax is reached with unexpected suddenness:

> But the day of the Lord shall come as a thief, in which the heavens shall pass away with great violence and the elements shall be melted with heat and the earth and the works which are in it shall be burnt up (2 PET 3:10).

Why this unexpected conclusion? It is because God was not waiting, but playing for souls. The moment He wins, the new world begins, and it becomes apparent to all ages that Christ's resurrection and the great general resurrection are like the morning and the evening of the same Easter, like the first and last thrust of the sickle into the same field of ripe corn.

IX

ETERNAL REST

THE THOUGHT OF REST seems to be the notion most universally associated with eternal life. Rest is the word found engraven on the tombstones of our cemeteries more frequently than any other expression of faith and hope. The most shadowy forms of Christianity still believe in rest for the departed, and make of this idea of rest the great contrast between mortal and supermortal conditions. The preference for the word "rest" in connection with the world to come is, of course, a sad reflection of the world that now is. For most men, no doubt, the climax of happiness presents itself to their imagination in the form of a complete deliverance from the conditions of life known to them on the present plane of existence. There is no human being so unimaginative as not to be impressed by that reversal of conditions implied in the ideas of rest and struggle. The silence that takes possession of the death-chamber where a human existence has tossed itself into calm rigidity, is powerfully suggestive of rest for the one who but a few moments before may have been writhing in agony, and the least religious will say that rest has come at last to the poor struggler. People who would never dare to say of their departed friends that they have gone to heaven, still say quite casually and without any awkwardness that their dear ones have gone to their rest.

The question may be asked here to what extent this visualizing of the Hereafter as a state of deep rest is consonant with Christian thought, or is the voice of the *anima naturaliter christiana* ("naturally Christian soul"). It is the purpose of this article to show that rest is the one quality predicated most constantly and most emphatically of the life of the world to come in Christian literature and Christian tradition. It would be a great comfort to anyone who loves nothing better than the dissemination of Catholic ideas to find this notion of eternal rest shared by most men:

So that by all means, whether by occasion or by truth, Christ be preached: in this also I rejoice, yea, and will rejoice (PHIL 1:18).

If Mrs. Grundy of Slumland were to come to me and tell me with the solemnity belonging to her kind that her man, the arch-ruffian of the lane, has gone to his rest (perhaps via the gallows), have I not found in Mrs. Grundy a kindred spirit? I, for one, should be very reluctant to make light of this remnant of solemnity and awe through which the most benighted minds look at a dead man as at one "who sleepeth," however grotesque the application of the Gospel phrase may appear in many a death-chamber.

To speak of the dead as of people who have found their rest, their eternal rest, is pure Christianity, though it is not the whole of Christianity. Outside Christianity you get the endless and restless migration of souls, you get the unhappy shades that wander through dank, dark, barren regions; you get rest with a vengeance in Buddhistic Nirvana, rest that means a total extinction, rest that is a separation from the wheel of existence, rest to be compared to the rest of the fly over which passes the wheel of a chariot. I am sure that Mrs. Grundy means something positive when she speaks of her dead husband's rest, though her power of discrimination between a positive and a negative notion may be extremely undeveloped. It is no small act of faith in the unseen world to take it for granted that the man who all his life has been more or less of a rebel against the oppressions of human conditions, has found his niche at last in the Beyond, where nothing provoke his ire, where the dark fires of resentment that were in his breast from his birth are finally extinguished. No doubt it is into some such paraphrase that our worthy friend of Slumland would expand her notion of rest in death, if she had time for verbal enlargements.

It would, of course, make an enormous difference if she added just one word, if she said over the dead man, as her Irish neighbour would be sure to say: "Eternal rest give unto him, O Lord"; this supplementary notion of rest being the gift of God, and consequently, being the object of man's prayer, is more than a theological nicety; it is the difference between old Christianity and new paganism. Does not neo-paganism claim all the fruits of Christianity and refuse to have any share in the sowing? Neo-paganism wants Christian happiness without the Christian tears; it asks for the risen life without the death on the Cross; it claims eternal rest without accepting any of the labour that precedes it. No one nowadays has any patience with the old paganism, with all its idols and vices, its cruelties and its slaveries. We are not even keen on its literature, which was its only saving grace. What people love is a paganism born of Christianity; they are all for the rest of the Christian heaven, but no mention ought to be made of the tears, of the mourning, of the crying, of the sorrow, that make the "former things" (Rev 21:4).

Now to say simply these words: "Eternal rest give unto him, O Lord," stamps Mrs. Murphy as a Christian, while her neighbour is no more than a neo-pagan when she says of her dead man: "He is at rest." She is not an infidel, she is not a pagan of the old sort, much less is she a Hindu or a Buddhist; but she is a neo-pagan; she is of the "last days" and of the "dangerous times" prophesied by St. Paul, when men shall be lovers of themselves, "having an appearance indeed of godliness but denying the power thereof" (2 Tim 3:5).

The rest which is the portion of God's saints in the world to come, according to Christian tradition, is not given by the physical cessation of life's energies. To be dead is not necessarily the same thing as to be at rest. The Liturgies of the Church, from the very dawn of Christianity, pray for the dead, and the burden of the prayer is the granting of rest and peace to the departed. This points to one thing, and to one thing only, that there is rest or unrest among the spirits themselves, that there is a state of peace and a state of discord in the spirit-world. Otherwise how would it be a rational prayer to intercede for the departed that eternal rest may be granted unto them? Is not that simple old practice of Catholicism to pray for the dead, to wish them rest and peace, an immense revelation of the unseen, showing us the spirit-world as a seething sea of unrest?

Human spirits go forth from the body on their wanderings, and when we thought that it was all stillness and quietness we are told that a people of spirits, numerous as the sand on the seashore, is tossed hither and thither in an elemental effort to find a center of stability, to reach a level of repose. Far from looking upon death as the goal where all yearnings cease, the Catholic Church seems to feel instinctively that the spirit of man is snatched up into a whirlpool of restlessness the moment it leaves the body, unless it be plunged straight into the great Pacific Ocean of beatific vision. How could the Church be so anxious about the eternal rest of the departed soul unless there were in her inner consciousness a haunting vision of struggling, yearning, thirsting souls, darting forward to the upper portion of the stream of life, as fish will seek to reach the stream that is above and behind the rocks, only to find that their efforts are nothing but a momentary illusion of success?

It is true to say that the death of the Christian ought to be perfect rest; ought to be synonymous with profoundest peace. The saint, the great ascetic, the martyr, in the language of the Church, finds rest in death. To such a one to die is to sit down under the shade of the trees of Eden. The consecrated word "rest" is not always a prayer on the lips of the Church; it is very often a sound of triumph. When a tomb in the Roman Catacombs has the words *In Pace* ("In Rest") inscribed upon it, they may signify the glories of martyrdom; the occupant is a hero to whom death is full and complete rest.

It would be an ideal Christianity if everyone who has faith in Christ were to long for the last hour of his life "as a servant longeth for the shade, as the hireling looketh for the end of his work" (JOB 7:2). Death ought to be a going home after a strenuous year of hard schooling. Did not our own good Cardinal Wiseman say quite simply that he greeted death as a schoolboy welcomes his holidays? What our neo-pagans say so indiscriminately of every worldling who has ceased from troubling, the Church says of her apostles, her martyrs; the Church would like to say it of all Christians who are carried to their graves, because it is truly in the power of most men who believe in Christ to be so consummated in faith and charity that to lay themselves down on their deathbed ought to be the same thing as entering upon their eternal rest. No doubt with many a fervent Catholic death is literally his blissful rest; perhaps this privileged condition is more frequent than we imagine. It is certain that this unhampered transition from the toils of the Christian arena to the repose of the blessed is an idea extremely familiar in the earlier literature of Christianity. In the *Dialogues* of St. Gregory the Great, for instance, the soul of many a Roman damsel, with just her fidelity to the Catholic faith to recommend her, is seen entering the heavenly mansion the moment her bodily eyes are closed in the sleep of death.

But all this supposes that the Christian's work has been done, and that it has been done well. For work not done, for bad, scamped work there is the fire of restlessness, not the cool breeze of the restful evening. The heat of midday toil goes on for the shirkers of all degrees.

> For other foundation no man can lay, but that which is laid: which is Jesus Christ. Now, if any man build upon this foundation, gold, silver, precious stones, wood, hay, stubble: Every man's work shall be manifest. For the day of the Lord shall declare it, because it shall be revealed in fire. And the fire shall try every man's work, of what sort it is. If any man's work abide, which he hath built thereupon, he shall receive a reward. If any man's work burn, he shall suffer loss: but he himself shall be saved, yet so as by fire (1 Cor 3:11-15).

Fire, not rest, is the portion of all those who have done bad work, though they be saved in their time, when there will be no more fuel for the fire. This is why we never cease to pray for the departed Christian, that rest may be granted to him.

Catholic imagination is well inspired when it pictures the purgation of disembodied Christian souls under all sorts of metaphors of toil, of heavy burdens, of big tasks to be done. It is simply another way of stating the postponement of the hour of rest. It matters little under which kind of symbolism that burden of the soul be presented to our imagination; the spirit of man has work to do, work that is overdue, work which was not done in the body, though it ought to have been then done. Till the neglected task be performed, the spirit of man, if it be a holy spirit, will exert itself in labors and struggles, that it may the sooner reach the goal from which it had strayed in negligence and indolence. Such a spirit will torment itself with its own efforts as with a fire, to make up for its delays when it walked the road to heaven in the body of mortal days. No truer, no better prayer could be formulated for the benefit of such a spirit than a prayer for rest.

Having thus given that inspiration for rest its true Christian setting, we may now drop all reservations and enjoy to the full the meaning of the *requies aeterna* ("eternal rest"). The great rest that is promised us in the life of the world to come is so near an approach to the manner in which God Himself has His being that we may be justified in saying that through it we share God's own personal privilege. Our inspired Scriptures speak of God as having a twofold phase of existence: the phase of work, and the phase of rest. The second phase, that of rest, is, in a way, a state of triumph and joy, which makes it a consummation of blessedness of a final character:

> So the heavens and the earth were finished, and all the furniture of them. And on the seventh day God ended his work which he had made: and he rested on the seventh day from all his work which he had done (Gen 2:1-2).

This rest of God is more than an anthropomorphic presentment of the mystery of creation: it is the function of God as the *Causa finalis* ("final cause"[2]) of all things, as creation is the function of God as *Causa effi-*

---

2 In the philosophy of St. Thomas, a final cause is the end for which an action is undertaken. The "end" is distinct from a mere "consequence" because it is properly causal, as a motive for action.

ciens ('efficient cause"[3]) of all things. In less learned terms, and without any Latin, let us say that God is, first, the Maker of all things, and that He is, secondly, the Goal of all things. As the Maker, He is described as being at work; as the Goal, He is represented as being at rest. It is only God who can be at the same time supreme Cause at both ends, so that all things come out from Him and all things go back to Him. This is the meaning of that Sabbath of God, the day of eternal rest:

> There remaineth therefore a day of rest for the people of God. For he that is entered into his rest, the same also has rested from his works, as God did from his (HEB 4:9-10).

No words could be more expressive in order to convey what rest means in Christian phraseology. We are meant to share God's eternal holiday. Not only do we receive gifts from Him: we also enter into His personal, into His private life, we follow that life in its twofold, infinite aspect in its work and in its rest.

It was to be expected that so wonderful a disclosure of God's moods as is contained in the second chapter of Genesis would not be left unexploited by the versatile genius of St. Paul. In the Epistle to the Hebrews he trounces the lazy, weak-kneed Christian in whom there is already "an evil heart of unbelief to depart from the living God" (HEB 3:12). St. Paul pictures God as turning upon such a one, as a father would upon the child that sulks on the road: "As I have sworn in my wrath: if he shall enter into my rest" (HEB 4:3). But I refrain from further comment on that glowing passage of St. Paul's Epistle to the Hebrews. Let me exhort my reader to take up the New Testament, carefully to read and analyze Chapters 3 and 4 of the Epistle, and fit into one mental picture God's sabbath after the six days of creation, the thirsty wanderings of thirty years' duration of the Jewish people, the rest of Jesus in death, and the repose of all

---

3 An efficient cause is the agent who performs an act by imparting form to the thing it acts upon.

His followers when their souls reach the promised land of heaven.

After reading St. Paul's brilliant theology we shall feel simply disgusted with the modern abuse of the beautiful word "rest" in relation to the Hereafter. Rest, in the Christian sense, is of all things the divinest, and we shall never again say the prayer, "Eternal rest give unto them," without being conscious of the immensity of our request. St. Paul's conclusion is, "Let us hasten therefore to enter into that rest" (HEB 4:11). We can never drop into it automatically, as a tired man drops into an armchair; we must run towards it with breathless haste.

Looking at this idea of eternal rest from the creature's point of view, one great impression is conveyed to our minds: this rest means a complete reversal of all the conditions of existence known to us. None of us really know what it means to have perfect rest associated with perfect consciousness of life. Our rests are suspensions of activities, interruptions in the flow of consciousness; our best rest is our sleep. God's rest is infinite wakefulness, an all-embracing contemplation of the work He has done. Such also will be the rest of His elect.

It means such continuance and such fullness of life that the very intensity of activity leaves no gap, no sign of a break, as one may watch a fast-revolving wheel without being able to see the movement so that one is tempted to lay one's fingers on the object as on a thing perfectly at rest, were it not for the warnings of the expert mechanic.

Far from us all such interpretations of the rest of our departed fellow-Christians, which savor more of narcotics than of faith in eternal life; which come from weariness of thought rather than from a desire to see good days. Eternal rest is unchanging contemplation of the beauties of God, not somnolency of the spirit. It is the joy of work, the exhilaration of eternal freshness of mind; it is work without fatigue, because it is the creature's best portion busy with the most perfect object; it is the fixity of the created mind on the uncreated Truth.

X

GOD'S POINT OF VIEW

THERE ARE TWO POWERS in each one of us which are as much a hindrance to our progress as they are a help. The two powers are imagination and sentiment. They are fine things in their own way, but they have a terrible knack of obstructing the higher, the more aristocratic powers of the soul: I mean the intellect and will. Philosophers, as a rule, are not humorists. Their bent of mind is rather rigid. But if a philosopher were as good a cartoonist as he is a solemn disputant he could start a comic paper with every chance of success, just with the object of pillorying the pranks played to our best and highest self by our sentimental and imaginative self.

A fine mind could be lampooned without injustice by being caricatured as tied to the tail of a grotesquely small imagination, full of diminutive legs and wings; whilst will-power could be seen in the shape of the mountain-man, Gulliver, led captive by an army of Lilliputian sentiments. Imagination and sentiment are very sweet handmaids, as long as they keep their own place. But they are a terrible nuisance, philosophically, to the master and the mistress upstairs if they begin talking in too provocative a key. St. Thomas Aquinas is a very polite writer, a most patient thinker and expounder of thought. He has a wonderful gift of suffering a fool gladly. Yet even he has his sighs when the detractor of Catholic thought shows an overwhelming bump of animal imagination. Then we hear him say, with a sigh, that such men are not fit to understand truth, because they are incapable of climbing to the top of their own imagination to see further afield: *non valentes transcendere imaginationem* ("not valiant in transcending imagination").

In this matter of eternal life, our two fickle faculties of imagination and sentiment often disturb the peace of the devoutest believer, making the spiritual hopefulness of many a good soul look grotesque. Imagination has a trick of representing eternal life as an endless boredom, whilst sentiment deflects the noble power of hope through an amazing interest taken in the fate of the reprobate. "I could never be happy in heaven," says sweet Miss Merciful, "if I were to know that there is even one tormented being in hell. I should feel every hour that I ought to go out of heaven and do something for that wretched creature." It would be a most sterile mission in the life of thought if one were tied down to the task of answering the perplexities of the imaginative and the hypersentimental. Such people are supremely unreasonable. I would not take up their challenge to reasonable faith if by doing so I did not gain the much-coveted opportunity of making more clear two very important features in the nature of the future life: unchangeableness of enjoyment and unlimited vision of truth.

Nothing could be less spiritual in its nature than the element of human time. "Time is money" is a modern, ill-savoring tag. Time is even less spiritual than mammon, since the fool and the wise alike may live an equal number of years, whilst a certain amount of prudence is always necessary to the acquisition and safe keeping of wealth. Is it not a bewildering spectacle to see the good and the wicked grow up, so to speak, into the same height of time, like so many trees, as if nature were determined to be supremely and serenely indifferent and impartial in this one thing, the duration of human lives? In all other things character will tell sooner or later; in this matter of the number of years allotted to men here on earth it is quite impossible to detect the least regard for individual merit. Bad men live fourscore years, so do good men; the inefficient grow to old age, so do the efficient. Men of intellect become greybeards, so do empty-headed gabblers. Innocent children are snatched away in the whiteness of their baptismal robe; the children of the outcast, with a hundred blemishes already tarnishing their souls, are reaped by death in their thousands, as were the Holy Innocents.

This great indifference of nature to mere numbers in the distribution of the days of our lives ought to be to us a very clear warning that in the things of the spirit there will be different standards and measures. The blessed life in heaven could never be considered as a succession of hours and days, otherwise there would not be any real privilege in that new life. We may experience some mental difficulty in getting rid of that heavy envelope of imagination that wraps so much of our thinking as if in swaddling clothes. Yet there can be no doubt at all as to the ephemeral character of the human time momentum. Whatever may be the life of the blessed, it could never be a mere succession of years. The spirit of the elect will not approach God and the things of God step by step, each movement being timed by the ever new second; on the contrary, the spirit of the elect will be carried right into the center of blessedness, where there is neither length nor shortness of duration, but where there is simply blessedness, and time is no longer:

> And the angel whom I saw standing upon the sea and upon the earth lifted up his hand to heaven. And he swore by him that liveth for ever and ever ... that time shall be no longer (Rev 10:5-6).

There have been self-analytical people who have counted those days of their life of which they could truly say that they have been happy days. A Mohammedan Caliph of Cordova, in the palmy days of Moorish splendor in Andalusia, left it in writing that his happy days amounted to just eleven. But if there is no longer any time measure, if there are no days, then happiness must needs be an unchanging possession. The very fact that we are still able to count happy hours and happy days is clear evidence that We are not in happiness, but that we approach towards happiness, as one ascends, one after another, the steps that lead up to a temple.

In our present condition we are first and foremost a thing divided into compartments of time divisions. These compartments, these hours, these days of ours, we try to fill up with happiness. Time is long and short as we are successful or unsuccessful in this our effort. But let happiness be our very life, our very condition of existence, no longer a thing borrowed from the outside, with no time compartments in our being to make happiness a piecemeal possession after all, then there can be neither shortage nor surfeit of bliss. We are simply happy through the very laws of our being, because we have our being in happiness, instead of having our being in time.

One never tires of quoting or hearing the old monastic legend of the monk and the bird, because no better thing has been said on the nature of heavenly joys than the lesson contained in the ancient lore. A robber baron, fearing the approach of the year one thousand and the end of the world, had taken the cowl in the poorest monastic foundation of his neighborhood. The dread of hell helped him over the hardest part of his new life. With the softening of the wild boar's nature, gentler visions arose in the primitive brain of the penitent. He bethought himself of heaven and its beauties. But there the tempter found a weak point for the attack. Heaven did not allure so mightily as hell had terrified. The robber baron, no doubt, remembered the tedious length of the entertainments which he sat out in the halls of his friends, how he had yawned when his host thought of diverting him. Would he not find even angelic music too monotonous to interest him forever? As the poor penitent was in solemn earnest about the future world, the subtle suspicion that had crept into his simple hope was beginning to poison his life. How would it be possible for God to do that thing, that a whole long eternity should never pall, should never lose its charm?

One day when he had been sent to gather wood in the forest, the insidious fear was gnawing at his heart more mercilessly than ever. He would do anything, he thought, for the man who would give him comfort in his sad perplexity. That very moment, however, all his attention was diverted to another object. A bird, high up in the branches of a tree, had started its song. The monk, overcome by the sweetness of that note—for the old robber baron was a poet at heart—ceased from his labor just for one moment, wondering whether there could be any sound more beautiful even in heaven. But soon the singer flitted away. Coming back to earth, the good man said that he could listen to such sounds for ever and ever, without fear of ennui. But a fresh surprise awaited him. On his return to the monastery gate he thought himself bewitched. There stood in front of him a noble abbey, with towers higher than the lofty tree from which the wonderful bird had been heard. Had he not left in the morning, when he sallied forth to his work, a house of earth and wattle, looking more like a stockade than the cloistered habitation of monks? Where did all this architectural magnificence come from? How had it all arisen between the hours of Prime and Vespers? The answer was given to the mystified penitent when he found himself in the midst of refined and courteous-looking monks, all strangers, all belonging as it were to another world. His ecstasy over the bird's song had lasted two centuries.

Our dear medievalists, who told such stories, were indeed wonderful men. They could clothe the same truth in garments as manifold as would be seen in a tournament of knights. The monastic chronicler with his legend of the singing bird said the same thing as the great meta— physicians of the period when they explained to keener intellects that time has no absolute value or worth, that it is a mere accidental thing, a by-product of nature, and that man would be admitted one day, through G0d's grace, to visualize all things *sub specie aeternitatis*, "from the angle of eternity"; and that in the glorious world to come we should not measure our happiness by days, but should rather take hold of happiness in its very essence, and, reversing roles, should measure duration by bliss, instead of measuring bliss by duration.

To be lifted up on the wings of God's eternity, to participate in God's mode of duration, as St. Thomas would have said, will be the great privilege

of the elect. But to enter into God's judgements will be a further refining of
the human mind for which there is no parallel, no legend in the history of
mankind. The elect will be made to see all things in the light of God. The
various events that shape the fate of rational creatures will be seen by the
glorified mind in a totally different relation. Such a mind will see things
and judge of things as God sees them and judges of them. Sentiment, if
there be any, will be entirely on the side of God. So far we have heard only
man pleading his own cause. How will it all look when God will show unto
us *His* case?

To people who protest that they could never be happy in a heaven from
which their next-of-kin would be excluded, the very pragmatic answer has
been given that whatever is not in heaven is better out of heaven, that a
husband in heaven need not be concerned about the wife who is not, because, when all has been said, she is better where she is. This, of course, is
true in a rough fashion. No reprobate would ever be happy in heaven, even
if he were put there by main force. One must be pure of heart to love the
vision of heaven.

But in reality we ought to rise to a higher and less geocentric range of
thought. We ought to profess frankly that God's judgements are holy, that
God's dealings with His rational creatures are infinitely just, and that the
elect, being admitted into the divine secrets, will emerge from the intimacy
entirely converted to the views of God, not to the opinion of the next-
of-kin. Every Christian has enough loyalty to God to make him believe
implicitly that God is supremely just and true in all His dealings with His
creatures of free-will. Yet here on earth this kind of loyalty is demanded
of us without any mitigation. In most matters we begin to see light long
before we are admitted to the vision of God; not so in this province of the
eternal fate of those that die in wickedness. We are far too much used to
viewing all things from the human center, even the divine dispensations.
We do not know what it is truly to sympathize with God, to see at a glance
what it means for God to be ill-used by His own free creatures.

Now the blessed in heaven will be essentially theocentric, not geocen-

tric. God will be their dearest father, their dearest mother, God will be to
them brother and sister. If there could be sadness in the bliss of heaven
the elect would be inconsolable over this, that the Supreme Beauty has
ever been despised by anyone. Beside such a sorrow, if it could exist, all
other sorrows would be as nothing. Sorrow there cannot be in the blessed
land. But is it not strange that certain sentimental people can actually ask
how they could ever be happy in heaven while there are reprobates outside
heaven, when it would be a much more pertinent question to ask how
it can ever be possible for us to rejoice in the Eternal Beauty without re-
morse, knowing, as we shall know, how long and how persistently we have
despised that Beauty? Surely it argues a great inversion of spiritual values
in man to speak of compassion for Satan and his followers, as if infinitely
greater wrong had not been done by us to God's majesty. The real, sentimental difficulty about eternal life ought to be this: how shall I ever be
happy in the presence of the All-Holy after such a life as mine? True Catholic sentiment is a compassionate feeling for Him whom we have pierced.
Is not purgatory an unceasing wail of the redeemed soul for the outraged
glory of God? Not a medievalist, but a modern of the modems, has sung
the soul's pity for the offended Divinity:

> When then—if such thy lot—thou seest thy Judge,
> The sight of Him will kindle in thy heart
> All tender, gracious, reverential thoughts.
> Thou wilt be sick with love, and yearn for Him,
> And feel as though thou couldst but pity Him,
> That one so sweet should e'er have placed Himself
> At disadvantage such, as to be used
> So vilely by a being so vile as thee.
> There is a pleading in His pensive eyes
> Will pierce thee to the quick, and trouble thee.
> And thou wilt hate and loathe thyself; for though
> Now sinless, thou wilt feel that thou hast sinned,

As never thou didst feel; and wilt desire

To slink away, and hide thee from His sight,

And yet Wilt have a longing aye to dwell

Within the beauty of His countenance.

And these two pains, so counter and so keen,

The longing for Him, when thou seest Him not;

The shame of self at thought of seeing Him,—

Will be thy veriest, sharpest purgatory.

(*Dream of Gerontius.*)

XI

THE WORLD OF GOD

ASA FURTHER CONTRIBUTION to these papers on eternal life we might lay stress on what I might legitimately call the cosmic meaning of the doctrine of heaven. Eternal life in the Catholic sense is essentially a world, a new world, the world of God. The saints of all degrees are a people, a mighty, an incomparably mighty race, the race of God, peopling in their bright multitudes the universe of which Christ is the King. The elect are not merely the chosen few safely housed in the inner chambers of God's abiding-place; they are, on the contrary, an imperial race, possessing the Whole mighty complex of the celestial spheres for their inheritance, and lording it over all things created. The world to come may be truly envisaged as the culmination of an almost endless process of progress and evolution from the day on which God created heaven and earth.

God made the human race in order visibly to embody some infinite ideal of beauty and perfection which He had in His mind from all eternity; no one single individual would suffice for a perfect embodiment of that ideal; countless millions are necessary in order to fill up, as it were, the ever-receding framework of that ideal. In other words, God wanted a people in the full sense of the concept, where all would have the same nature, the same essential qualities, and who, at the same time, would constitute, in their untold multitudes, one moral personality. Spirits could not truly constitute a people, as their individualities are far too pronounced to coalesce into anything like one race. A people is one in many and many in one. This was God's idea when He created mankind—to have a divine people; the world to come is therefore above all things the world of God's people, with a King at the head of it, Christ Jesus.

The enemy of God swore in the darkness of his heart that God should never succeed in getting together a people all His own; the very element of multitudinousness, which is the essential element of a people, gave the proud Spirit his chance; how would it ever be possible to keep in oneness of love and purpose human beings more numerous than the stars in heaven, than the grains of sand on the sea-shore? Their individual liberties could never be tuned to the uniform pitch of one vast act of love. Would it not he, even for God, a thing beyond realization, that beings, practically infinite in number, should he one heart and one soul, that necessary condition for the existence of any people, truly so-called?

With irresistible purpose, born of profoundest hatred, Satan is pursuing his work of breaking up the human race, so as to render the idea Of the One people of God a practical impossibility. Looking at the human race in its present and in its past, will ever anyone but a dreamer conceive of the human race as one people, much lees as the people of God? The success of the spirit of hatred seems overwhelming, the failure of God's plan seems complete, the ruination looks final, absolute.

Now is it not the very mystery of the world to come that under the ruins of the first plan of God there lies hidden a structure of supreme magnificence and completeness of design? God *has* Hie people after all, and not one of His Original schemes has miscarried.

If we once adopt this view of the divine people, With a life and a mission worthy of God, We Shall love Our Scriptures best in their literal meanings, and the immensity of the present world's history, far from overwhelming us, will appear to be a thing of perfect proportions.

Numbers are the blessing of a people; making the merciful hypothesis that all, or nearly all, human beings ever born, who lived and died on this earth, are saved, there would not be too many for the people of God. For such a people, to be worthy of its appellation, would be numbered, not in human, but in divine arithmetic. With this simple and majestic concept of the people of God, number, far from being oppressive, becomes the glory of the mind and the joy of the heart. See how St. John relished that idea of number in the people of God:

> After this, I saw a great multitude, which no man could number, of all nations and tribes and peoples and tongues, standing before the throne and in sight of the Lamb, clothed with white robes, and with palms in their hands (REV 7:9).

The vision of that coming people was the solace of Christ in the darkest hour of His Passion:

> There shall be declared to the Lord a generation to come: and the heavens shall show forth his justice to a people that shall be born, which the Lord hath made (Ps 21:32).

These words are the last verse of the Psalm intoned on the Cross by the Son of God Himself:

> About the ninth hour, Jesus cried with a loud voice, saying: *Eli, Eli, lamma sabacthani?* That is, My God, my God, why hast thou forsaken me (MATT. 27:4-6)?

The whole stellar world is not too vast for the activities of a nation whose mission will be to render perfect service unto God. Catholic theology begins its work by laying down a few immutable and fixed principles in this matter of the life of the world to come; absolute sinlessness of the human will, unchangeability of the state of sanctity, the clear vision of God by the human intellect, the re-establishment of the total human personality, and intercourse with the heavenly spirits, are certain and unchallenged truths, the highest peaks of that world to come which we see even from this earth in the light of faith. But such dogmatic fixtures are far from being an imprisonment of thought, they are—to change my metaphor—the guiding buoys for our navigation. Nothing prevents our visualizing the mighty host of the elect human race as developing untold powers of activity with a freedom of will and resourcefulness of genius unknown to the sons of Adam while they dwell on this planet; their liberty—shall we say their initiative—will be heightened to an unknown power; and may we not think of them as doing things truly worthy of a race of giants for the glory of God and His Christ?

The supreme and active dominion of the human race over every kind of wickedness is a favorite idea with St. Paul: " Know you not that the saints shall judge this world" (1 COR 6:2)? Is not this vision also the swan-song of Isaiah:

> For as the new heavens and the new earth, which I will make to stand before me, saith the Lord: so shall your seed stand, and your name. And there shall be month after month and sabbath after sabbath: and all flesh shall come to adore before my face, saith the Lord. And they shall go out and see the carcasses of the men that have transgressed against me. Their work shall not die and their fire shall not be quenched: and they shall be a loathsome sight to all flesh (ISA 66:22-24).

There is in St. Luke's Gospel a delightful antithesis between this present world and the next, where Christ, in contrasting the conditions of the two, evidently insinuates the truth that the future world will be as active a field of life as the present one:

> The children of this world marry and are given in marriage: but they that shall be accounted worthy of that world and of the resurrection from the dead shall neither be married nor take wives. Neither can they die any more: for they are equal to the angels

and are the children of God, being the children of the resurrection (Luke 20:34-36).

A day will come when it will be made apparent to all creatures that God has *not* failed with mankind: that man, far from being a disappointment to Him, is His supreme glory. The human race will be the brightest jewel in the crown of the King of the ages; many individual human beings may have been failures, the race itself is a splendid success.

Nowhere have God's wisdom and God's power been shown with such splendor as in the infinitely wise use which He has made of the ruins of the human race. This reconstruction is the burden of all prophecies. In the words of St. Peter, the Son Himself is awaiting that supreme event in heaven:

> The times of refreshment shall come from the presence of the Lord: and he shall send him who hath been preached unto you, Jesus Christ, whom heaven indeed must receive, until the times of the restitution of all things, which God hath spoken by the mouth of his holy prophets, from the beginning of the world (Acts 3:20-21).

Christ will be the King of that new people, and from the excellency of the Sovereign may we not conclude also the greatness of the nation He commands? What will not mankind do under such a leader?

> For the Lamb, which is in the midst of the throne, shall rule them and shall lead them to the fountains of the Waters of life: and God shall wipe away all tears from their eyes (Rev 7:17).

Well-meaning people, not excluding the Apostles, often ask the question whether many are saved. We know Christ's way of evading the query. In our own day this concern about numerical salvation is very keen, but, through the actual nature of the case, it leads nowhere; whether there be many lost or few, the main claim of Christianity is not affected by it. Christianity claims that through the Incarnation mankind has been made safe for God. Since His Son became a member of the human race there is no other perdition than individual perdition. Man's fall in Eden was universal perdition; this has been irrevocably made right through the redemption.

Concern about the fate of individual people, without remembering the great fact of mankind's redemption as a race, might lead us into very superficial modes of thought. One thing is as certain as anything can be certain in Christian doctrine: God's victory over man's enemy, Satan, is a final victory.

XII

THE RESURRECTION OF THE BODY

HERE IS NO EXPRESSION more frequently used in the Holy Scriptures than the expression "resurrection of the dead." To raise up the dead is the unmistakable sign of divine power. Very often this supreme effect of heavenly omnipotence is called resurrection from the dead, as if there were a vast kingdom of beings, the dead, which now and then yields up some of its denizens to that other kingdom of beings, the living, at the voice of those who speak in the Name of God.

We may, in spite of the frequency with which the resurrection of the dead is mentioned in the inspired books, reduce to three classes the various resurrections known to Christian revelation. There are first those resurrections in which the human body, or, if you prefer it, the corpse, is in presence of the *thaumaturgus* ("wonder-worker"), and the dead man is seen to rise, is heard to speak. In the second place there is Christ's own return to life, in virtue of His own power, and His return to life means a prodigious increase of perfection and felicity to Himself; it means a happy life: He not only rises from the dead, He rises from death to glory. Thirdly, we have the clear announcement of a resurrection from the dead entirely different from the two kinds already spoken of, at least in external appearance. It is the coming back to full human conditions of every individual of our race, at the end of the world, *ex cineribus,* "from the dust," from the scattered elements, from the unseen, when there will not be even a corpse into which to pour life.

We may, for this last kind of resurrection, assume that all human bodies will be reduced to the invisible elements before the resurrection takes place. This apparent nothingness is indeed the normal starting-point for that third class of resurrection which is guaranteed to us by our Christian faith. It is quite permissible for a Catholic to hold that the great world-conflagration, when "the elements shall be melted with heat and the earth and the works which are in it shall be burnt up" (2 PET 3:10), will precede the general resurrection of the dead. St. Thomas Aquinas, for one, holds to this sequence of the eschatological events.[4] It just shows how very little our theology depends on any preservation of "relics" for its defense of the third kind of resurrection, the resurrection from the " ashes."

I need not spend much time in pointing out to the reader how different are the characteristics of the three sorts of resurrection known to our faith. Lazarus, the friend of Christ, may stand as the pattern of the first kind of resurrection. The grave is opened by the hands of an expectant crowd; Christ cries with a loud voice: "Lazarus, come forth" (JOHN 11:43). Lazarus comes forth "bound feet and hands with winding bands," and Christ gives this peremptory command: "Loose him and let him go" (JOHN 11:44). How different is that other resurrection, the resurrection of the first Easter, the coming back of Christ to life. Christ rises in His own power; His body, though inanimate, had never seen a moment's corruption; unlike the body of the brother of Martha—was not Martha terrified at the thought that her brother might be made to come out of the grave?—Christ's body passes through the sepulcher as a ray of light passes through crystal. Then there is the third resurrection, without a corpse at all over which to call: "Come forth." For truly mankind will be nowhere at the instant that will precede the general resurrection.

---

4   *ST,* Supp. q. 74, a. 7

It is to my mind a thing of immense significance that the same form of words is used to express three things so very different in all but one point, the finding of bodily life after the loss of bodily life. It will suffice here to quote Christ's own phrases in order to show how the expression " to rise from the dead " is applied indiscriminately to the three kinds of resurrection known to Christian thought. To the disciples of John, Christ enumerates the visible and evident signs of His divine power:

> Go and relate to John what you have heard and seen. The blind see, the lame walk, the lepers are cleansed, the deaf hear, the dead rise again, the poor have the gospel preached to them (MATT 11:4-5).

Here we have the rising of the dead mentioned as a thing that was evidently a common occurrence in Christ's public ministry. Of His own resurrection Christ speaks, one might almost say, in the same casual way:

> And as they came down from the mountain, Jesus charged them, saying: Tell the vision to no man till the Son of man be risen from the dead (MATT 17:9).

The third kind of return to bodily life, the last resurrection, so different from the others, is still spoken of by the Son of God in the same easy strain:

> And as concerning the dead that they rise again have you not read in the book of Moses, how in the bush God spoke to him, saying: I am the God of Abraham and the God of Isaac and the God of Jacob? He is not the God of the dead, but of the living (MARK 12:26-27).

This persistent use on the part of Christ of the identical words for every kind of resurrection is a clear evidence that in the Gospel there is no mention of a resurrection which is not a bodily resurrection. The dead that rose under the eyes of Christ's followers are the pattern of what resurrection from the dead means, both in Christ's own case and in the case of mankind generally at the end of the world's history. It has been asserted that Christ could never speak of a bodily resurrection in connection with the general resurrection of the human race; that the very words He used, and which we quoted just now from St. Mark, point clearly to a merely spiritual meaning of the resurrection.

Such is the main thesis of a recent publication by Dr. H.D.A. Major, Principal of Ripon Hall, Oxford, *A Resurrection of Relics*, in which the writer tries to prove that he himself is quite an orthodox believer in resurrection, without holding the doctrine of a bodily resurrection, because, says he, Christ Himself never went really beyond the announcement of a spiritual resurrection for mankind at the end of time.

Commenting on the passages from the Synoptic Gospels, where our Lord deals *ex professo* ("explicitly") with the resurrection of the last day, and which I have just quoted, Dr. Major says:

> Here Christ rejects as inadequate the old habitual view held by the Sadducees that there was no resurrection, and that the dead exist in a gloomy underworld in exile from God; but at the same time He decisively rejects the materialistic view of the resurrection taught in Daniel and the later Apocalyptists; and He clearly affirms that lofty conception of the resurrection which is expressed with such spiritual emotion in the Book of Wisdom. This is the only passage in the Gospels which clearly indicates the precise nature of our Lord's teaching about the resurrection, but it is adequate.[5]

Yet, is there anything more arbitrary than to attach all at once an entirely new significance to a form of words which on all other occasions mean something very clear, very definite? To raise up the dead stands for a physical fact, all over the Synoptic Gospels—to confine ourselves to that portion of Holy Writ—the bringing back of life into a dead body. "Heal the sick, raise the dead, cleanse the lepers, cast out devils. Freely you have

---

5   Major, *Resurrection of Relics*, p. 77

received, freely give" (MATT 10:8), such was our Lord's clear and practical injunction to the disciples. Are we to suppose, then, that when He speaks in their presence of a further resurrection from the dead, of His own, of mankind in general, He attaches to the same words a meaning completely different, that He makes the time-honored words to stand for an idea so entirely alien to all their religious education? They were given power to raise the dead, they saw their Master raise the dead; all raising up of the dead was to them, as to everyone else, a coming back to bodily life. The words had no other significance. Believers and unbelievers attached the same idea to the same words:

> At that time Herod the Tetrarch heard the fame of Jesus. And he said to his servants: This is John the Baptist: he is risen from the dead: and therefore mighty works show forth themselves in him (MATT 14:1).

If space allowed we might analyze the Acts of the Apostles and the Epistles with the same end in view of finding out how the same form of words must mean the same thing, a resurrection of such a nature as was comprehensible to all men, such as all men understood, a bodily resurrection. The evidence would be overwhelmingly in favor of our taking literally the old phrase, whether it be applied to Peter's act of restoring life to the dead Tabitha, when "Peter, kneeling down, prayed, and turning to the body he said: Tabitha, arise" (ACTS 9:40); whether it be the profession of faith in Christ's return from death, or the announcement of the great judgement, "when the dead shall hear the voice of the Son of God" (JOHN 5:25).

Dr. Major quotes with approval some lines of Locke, in which the English philosopher defends his own lack of belief in a bodily resurrection:

> In the New Testament ... I find our Savior and the Apostles to preach the *resurrection of the dead*, and the *resurrection from the dead*, in many places. But I do not remember any place where the

resurrection of the same body is so much as mentioned: nay, what is very remarkable in the case, I do not remember in any place of the New Testament (where the general resurrection of the last day is spoken of) any such expression as the resurrection of the body, much less of the same body.[6]

Locke's contention that there is no such expression as "the resurrection of the body" in the New Testament is, of course, correct, though we have many passages in the New Testament where the rising of the body is expressly mentioned in connexion with the resurrection of the dead. But even if we had no such clear scriptural allusion to the body's share in the final resurrection, the very idea of a rising of the dead implies for every New Testament authority, be it Christ, be it His Apostles, be it their entourage, a bodily revival. When St. Paul, speaking in presence of Festus, the Roman Governor, and King Agrippa and Berenice, thus apostrophises his very worldly audience, "Why should it be thought a thing incredible that God should raise the dead?" (ACTS 26:8) everybody knew what he meant, and if St. Paul, as Locke would have it, had understood by resurrection merely some mysterious transformation of the spirit of man, he would have been guilty of downright juggling with ideas in presence of people who could attach only one meaning to his words.

These burning words of St. Paul furnish me with the opportunity of passing from the exegetical part of my theme to the physical possibility of the resurrection of the body, and indeed of the same body. Dr. Major would have us believe that the modern man is adverse to the doctrine of a bodily resurrection, not so much as a follower of Darwin or Tyndall or Huxley and the other materialists, but as a reader of the learned scholars who have found out for us that Christ could never mean bodily resurrection when He spoke of the rising up of the dead.[7] This is sheer bunkum.

---

6   John Locke, *An Essay Concerning Human Understanding*, Book I, chap. 27
7   Major, *Resurrection of Relics*, p. 72

Men recoil from the physical miracle implied in the universal resurrection of mankind; then they proceed, if they are Anglican divines, to prove that the Son of God could never mean things literally.

St. Paul's interrogation: "Why should it be thought a thing incredible that God should raise the dead ?" is a challenge to human incredulity which still awaits an answer. There is no doctrine in our Christian belief which is a more logical outcome of that generally admitted principle of all theism, the infinitude of God's power and knowledge. If God has truly infinite energy, combined with omniscience, the resurrection of the dead, in their identical bodies, becomes part of our belief in God's creative power. The resurrection, even the general resurrection, is not a mystery in the way in which the doctrines of the Trinity or the Incarnation or the Eucharist are mysteries. That a power that is infinite should not be able to raise up the dead would be the strangest illogicalness.

I cannot help feeling that in our treatment of the theology and philosophy of the resurrection there is one element which we leave out of sight to an extent which positively confuses the issues. Resurrection means, above all things, restoration of life, continuation through God's act of that life which had been interrupted by death. The dead are made to live again:

> And as in Adam all die, so also in Christ all shall be made alive. But everyone in his own order: the firstfruits, Christ: then they that are of Christ, who believed in his coming (1 COR 15:22-23)?

The risen Christ had evidently the same life before and after His resurrection. It is true that the life after the resurrection had qualities of glory which the life before the crucifixion did not possess. Yet substantially it is the same life, before and after. He laid down His life for us, and He took it up again for us. The everlasting meritoriousness of Christ's mortal career lies in this, that now, in His risen state, there pulsates in Him that very life which He took from His blessed Mother. It would not be enough to say that Christ in His resurrection took back the same soul and the same body; He took back the same life, that life which had ceased to flow when He gave up the ghost.

The resuscitated Lazarus was given back his life; after the great miracle at the tomb Lazarus lived as he had lived before. He knew himself to be the same as he had always been; the whole power of his resurrection lay in this, that none of the life which he had enjoyed before his death was lost to him. He had the same memories, the same experiences, the same habits of mind and body, the same physical constitution, the same development of powers as if there had been no sort of interruption. Death with regard to God, "who quickeneth the dead, and calleth those things that are not, as those that are" (ROM 4:17), can never be more than the state of sleep. In raising up the dead, He brings them back to that consciousness which was part of their former lives, and the risen ones are like men awaking from a long sleep:

> But he (Jesus) said: Weep not. The maid is not dead, but sleepeth. And they laughed him to scorn, knowing that she was dead. But he taking her by the hand, cried out, saying: Maid, arise. And her spirit returned: and she arose immediately. And he bid them give her to eat (LUKE 8:52-55).

It is a thing of deep significance that even with regard to the last resurrection, the resurrection from the dust, the dead are called sleepers by Holy Writ:

> For if we believe that Jesus died and rose again: even so them who have slept through Jesus, will God bring with him (THESS 4:13).

By all the principles of Catholic psychology, the human beings who have been in their graves for a thousand years are neither nearer to nor farther away from life than was the daughter of Jairus, who had died just before Jesus arrived in the house. To believe in God's power to raise up the dead man whose corpse still forms an apparent, cohesive whole, and to hesitate in one's belief in God's power to raise to life those whose ashes have been scattered to the winds, would be almost childish illogicalness.

To divine omniscience it cannot matter where the ultimate elements of man's natural self are to be found. The return to life of a dead body is equally possible or impossible whatever the state or condition of that body, whatever the degree of disintegration.

Is not death this very thing, the final unfitness of a bodily organism for life? A corpse is as distant from the source of life as the ashes inside a funeral urn, and whosoever is in the grave may be said to be only a sleeper with regard to God's omnipotent power to restore life, as it is no more difficult for God to give life to the dead of ancient date than to the son of the widow who is just being carried to his grave.

We have St. Paul's authority for saying that the bodies of the innumerable Christians who are in their graves will be raised to life as easily as the dead body of Christ, who is only "the first fruits of them that sleep" (1 Cor 15:20). To my mind the question of the resurrection of the dead is wonderfully simplified if once we grasp clearly this idea of the restoration of the personal life which ceased to flow when death supervened.

In order to make this point of view clearer, let us define here what is meant by life. We may consider in man two extremes, the spiritual principle and the material principle. The spiritual principle is called soul. It is created directly by God in every case, when man is conceived in his mother's womb. The material principle may be called the atomic or molecular elements that are at the basis of the matter that enters evidently into man's composition. It is of no importance whatever, for our purpose, to enumerate the various theories on the ultimate constituents of matter. Provided we hold that there is a real and radical difference between matter and spirit, the Catholic thinker may follow any school he likes for his theories on the ultimate physical constitution of matter.

Now life is neither the spiritual element in man, the soul, nor the material, the atomic element: life is something between these two elements, something that is neither spirit nor matter, but a wonderful blending of the two. I speak here of human life, as it is the only life relevant to my purpose. At death neither of the two extremes in man is destroyed, but life is completely destroyed. The spiritual element, the soul, still exists in virtue of its own innate permanence, as a spiritual being; likewise the atomic elements remain forever. Of the spiritual element, the soul, we say that it is immortal; we use no such word with regard to the atomic elements, though they be everlasting in their own way.

The term "immortal" applied to man's spiritual element is hallowed by tradition. But for the metaphysical mind it is not the best term. It implies a comparison with the body; it is a relative term to convey the truth that the soul of man does not break up like the body at death. Considered in itself, the soul is a simple being, an elementary thing of the spiritual order, as atoms, or whatever you may call them, are simple elements of the material order.

Is life, then, the union between the two elements, the spiritual and the material, between the soul and the first material principles? No scholastic who understands the true nature of the union between spirit and matter would say such a thing. Life is not the union between spirit and matter in man; life is something that is both a preparation for that union and a result of that union. The soul is not united with dead matter, but with living matter, and the union in its turn becomes a higher accentuation of life. Life is caused in matter, in the first instance, not by a soul, but by God, the Creator of all life, or by the living parent that generates life. The soul fosters life, enlarges life, carries life to wonderful heights in man, but does not create or cause life, vivifying, as it were, inanimate matter. God alone can give life to matter which is still inorganic. The soul could never be the effective cause of life, though it be a principle of life in another way.

Need I apologize to my reader for introducing him to these considerations of rational psychology? Is not the threefold distinction between the spiritual principle, the material principle, and life, the very key to all theology on the resurrection of the dead? The spirit is never destroyed, but life is destroyed, and life is the one thing which every resurrection from the dead restores. Death is not primarily a separation between spirit and matter in man; death is the extinction of life—this may sound like a tautology—and the spirit, i.e. the soul, departs because there is no life. So, likewise, the resurrection is not *primarily* the reunion of spirit and matter;

it is *primarily* the restoration of life. The reunion of a spirit and a matter is, of course, indispensable to the resurrection, because spirit and matter are indispensable to life: but they are not the resurrection phenomena, just as their separation is not the death phenomenon. Departure of life and return of life are death and resurrection from the dead respectively.

I am avoiding studiously the term "body" in the considerations that I am here propounding to the reader. The word "body" is, to a great extent, a metaphorical expression, whilst the term "matter" is a literal expression. The human body is matter that has life, and after all has been said, human body and human life are identical in meaning. A corpse is not a body, but dead matter. The human body is matter that has life, highly organized life, and has wonderful workings of the highest order.

I am afraid we are all of us deeply ignorant of the excellence of that much-scorned portion of our being, the body; and that we think of it in terms of *avoirdupois* ("bodily wieght") rather than in terms of psychology. Yet the body is all our human life. It is not, it is true, a spirit life, which deals in universals, which has freedom of choice; but, for all practical purposes of philosophy, it may be said that body and life in man are the same thing, and that the body is truly this wonderful middle between the spiritual element and the material element in man, or, to speak a language less startling, bodily life is that middle.

It may seem strange at first sight that there should be made a distinction between body and matter. Yet this distinction is essential to our understanding of man's nature, and of all those doctrines that are connected with theories on man's nature; and if anything is forever interwoven with speculation on man's nature it is the resurrection of the dead; the nature of man on the one side, and the divine omnipotence on the other, are the *rationale* of all our defense of the famous dogma. This distinction, then, between the body of man and matter will be easily admitted if, instead of the word "body" we use the word "sense" Our body is the totality of our sense activities. Our body means as much as the realm of our sense activities. Now, what is the extent of that realm? To what height, to what depths does sense activity reach in man? Be it said at once, the workings inside a human individual that are sense operations, and therefore are the body, are numerous beyond computation, marvellous beyond description.

I feel at this moment that the proper way of treating the whole doctrine of the resurrection of the flesh would be to write an exhaustive treatise on the extent of sense life in man. It is the only thing that matters here besides our faith in God's creative power. But I must ask my reader to take much for granted. As a sufficiently comprehensive statement of the case let me put the matter thus: in man there are never any workings, even of the highest and the purest order, without the help of sense activity, and most of man's workings are sense activities pure and simple, though of a very excellent degree, of an immensely more refined and penetrating nature than anything that is found in even the most perfectly developed animals. Death completely destroys all this, whilst it leaves intact the spiritual element of man and abandons matter to its own laws. Resurrection from the dead is the act of God by which He gives back that very thing, the whole glorious realm of sense activity, which had ceased to be.

Unstinted and complete restoration of all the sense life that makes us human beings is the true and primary meaning of the resurrection of the body; this is how the dead are made to live again.

Moreover, if the resurrection of a dead man means anything, we must admit, as already insinuated, that this body, or, if you prefer, this bodily life, must be the bodily life that came to a standstill at death. Every fiber in the risen man must tell him that he is the one who loved and hated, and enjoyed and suffered. The whole ethical merit of the resurrection turns on this absolute identity and oneness of bodily life:

> For we must all be manifested before the judgement seat of Christ,
> that every one may receive the proper things of the body, according
> as he has done, whether it be good or evil (2 Cor 5:10).

The historic resurrections, like the resurrection of Lazarus, are our best guidance in judging of the power of God's life-giving energy. We know little of that friend of Christ, Lazarus; but suppose him, for the sake of argumentation, to have been a man of great artistic or poetical accomplishments; say, even a musical genius, with a wonderful store of memories in harmony: then by the very terms of the resurrection privilege that was to be his, all that he ever knew or had learnt was given back to him when he came forth from the grave. Had his memory, his powers, been less active in the second, the miraculous, portion of his life, his death would have left a sad mark on him.

But why deal in suppositions? Have we not the most authentic instance in Christ Himself? Death could never impair the spirit, the soul of Christ. On the contrary, in the words of St. Peter, being put to death indeed in the flesh, He was "enlivened in the spirit" (1 PET 3:18). Yet in His death was an immense immolation; it was the cessation of that human life of His which is the marvel of God's creation. All that great activity of His bodily organism was extinguished; His brain ceased to work, His heart ceased to throb, His imagination went out like the beam of a lighthouse that collapses suddenly. That portion was truly destroyed. It was nowhere to be found; there were no remnants of it anywhere. It is of this we speak as Christ's great sacrifice; and though the cessation of that great life was of short duration, in the words of St. Thomas Aquinas, even a temporary cessation of so excellent a thing was a greater loss than man can conceive.[8]

At the resurrection it all came back, and Christ stood before His disciples with the marks of His physical wounds; but the life itself bore no signs of interruption; impossible to detect anything there which would have betrayed the cutting asunder of the thread of natural activities. He was the same, with all past memories and affections in full swing:

> And he said to them: Why are you troubled, and why do thoughts arise in your hearts? See my hands and feet, that it is I myself. Handle, and see: for a spirit hath not flesh and bones, as you have seen me to have. And when he had said this he showed them his

---

8   *ST*, III, q. 46, a. 6, ad 4

hands and feet. … And he said to them: These are the words which
I spoke to you while I was yet with you, that all things must needs
be fulfilled which are written in the law of Moses and in the proph-
ets and in the psalms, concerning me (LUKE 24:38-40, 44).

How, then, is this identical life restored at the resurrection? There is
only one answer: through God's omnipotence. In all resurrection there is
this double aspect of God's active power: He produces a life that is not, and
He unites the elements, spiritual and material, that are. Not to keep these
two workings of the divine power separate has led to endless confusion of
thought in this matter of the resurrection.

The spiritual soul of man cannot be united with dead matter, but only
with a living organism. The coming of the soul, say, to the corpse of Lazarus, could never vivify that corpse. This would grant the soul an effective
causality of life, whereas it only possesses a formal causality of life, as the
schoolmen say. God, by a direct act of His, had to quicken the corpse when
He united the soul with it; had to reconstruct, out of the treasures of His
omnipotence, the life which had been destroyed and whose destruction
had meant the soul's departure. Nor could the spiritual soul give back to
the corpse of Lazarus all the memories, the sensations, the associations of
experience which have their seat in the complicated organism of sense life.
God alone can restore life that is extinct; the soul cannot do it.

Here, again, I feel that my subject would be best served by an elabo-
rate study on the nature of the union between soul and body in man. But
I must crave the indulgence of my readers, and beg of them to trust my
knowledge of the Catholic philosophy of the human soul.

Great as the soul is, it cannot cause matter to live, to feel, to have
perceptions and loves and memories, when matter is mere dead matter.
Inside living matter the soul does wonders; on dead matter the soul cannot operate. Now matter is living matter either through natural generation
from a living parent or through God's act, "who quickeneth all things"
(1 TIM 6:13).

So to put the final conclusion of all we have said: in every resurrection there is the direct act of God producing a life that is no longer in any shape or form, and making it to be the identical life that once was. This is the true and central marvel of the resurrection. The identity of bodily life, and therefore the identity of our bodies in the resurrection, taking the term "body" as distinguished from the term " matter," has only one source, the omnipotence of God, who can make these things to be again that have vanished from the realms of being, that have ceased to be. To what extent, then, is it necessary that the soul of man and the atomic matter that was once in the body should be brought together again in order to have the resurrection of the same individual? That there could be no true resurrection without the identical spirit or soul that was in man before death being brought back into intimate association with all that life which I have described, and which is the direct product of God's vivifying power, seems to be an obvious truth. All that great life, on the one hand, ministers to the spiritual element in man, and, on the other hand, is constantly influenced by it. It could never be the same life again unless the same soul were given again as the psychic centre of it all, in a wonderful play of mutual influence, of action and reaction.

I shall presently make a few remarks on the true role of the soul in man, as I fear more than one reader might accuse me of belittling the soul's position in man's personality by calling it, as I have consistently done, man's spiritual element, instead of giving it the full control of man's existence. No one seems to experience any difficulty, unless he be a downright materialist, in granting this return of the identical soul in the resurrection. The tendency has been the other way, to give the soul such a role as to make resurrection ethically superfluous and psychologically inexplicable, precisely because people have not made the very important distinction on which everything turns, the distinction between the soul of man and the life of man, as I am doing in this paper. Certainly, if the soul were man's complete life there would be no need for any kind of resurrection.

We now come to the most vexed portion of my subject, the identity of the atomic matter—such, I think, is still the best way of expressing it—in the risen body and in the body before death. To admit this identity seems to many too exacting a tax on their reasoning powers. In fact, all controversy seems to hinge on that one point, whether it is at all defensible or reasonable that the same atomic matter should enter into the risen organism as entered into the mortal organism. Yet to me it seems that, if once we grant the absolute identity of life, the identity of the atomic matter is a small thing to accept. If that atomic matter exists individually, then God must know where to find it; if it does not exist in any separate individuality, there is no reason why we should insist on its being used in building up the risen life. Provided we have the identity of life, the identity of the atomic matter becomes a secondary consideration.

But all we know of resurrection has this feature, identity of matter in the two states, the natural state and the risen state, as in the miracles of the Gospel and the resurrection of Christ. So the whole tendency of the Church's mind is in favor of the same identity of matter in the universal resurrection. But, let us say it quite frankly, our doctors consider this identity to be of secondary importance; they even admit of exceptions. A very grave schoolman, of the most orthodox type, usually known as Ferrariensis, the best elucidator of the *Summa Contra Gentes* of St. Thomas, is explicit in teaching that there is no reason other than God's good pleasure why the matter, which he calls the ashes, which at one time entered into the formation of the human body, should be restored to the same body; the matter itself has no special affinity with any organism, but it is a fitting thing that the same matter should enter into the same life again. I quote the profound schoolman in his Latin text, as such words are a great acquisition to Catholic thought:

> *Videtur autem hoc esse de mente St. Thomae . . . quod in cineribus a quibus fiet resurrectio, nulla est naturalis inclinatio ad resurrectionem, sed solum ex ordine divinae providentiae statuentis illos cineres iterum animae conjungi debere.*

[This, however, seems to be the mind of St. Thomas ... that in the dust from which the resurrection will be, nothing is naturally inclined to resurrection, but only by the order of divine providence declaring that that dust ought again to be conjoined to a soul.][9]

Let us take note of these liberal views of great theologians, making of the return of the same elementary material thing, not an indispensable necessity without which there could be no true resurrection, but a generous ordering of God's providence, watching over man's substance in the "lower parts of the earth" (Ps 138:15). But to doubt God's knowledge and power to bring together the dust of which we were once made, is indeed to abdicate every principle of theodicy.

We have therefore to consider a threefold identity in the risen human being, which makes him the same human person he was from his birth: identity of soul, identity of bodily life, identity of the ultimate material elements. Of these three, the first is easily granted by all save by the materialists; the second is the very heart of the resurrection marvel, the most wonderful achievement of God's omnipotence; the third is the general rule of all resurrection in God's present providence, but it is not easily perceived to what degree this third identity is necessary to the reconstruction of the human person. Matter—i.e. a thing, an element that is not spirit—belongs to man's nature even when that nature stands at the right hand of God, as does the risen Christ. So no Catholic could ever hold the opinion that there could be a resurrection without material elements; if questionings are allowed, the hesitation is merely about the identity of those elements.

A discussion on the resurrection of the dead must needs give rise to endless queries, since this one doctrine has direct affinities with every other Christian dogma. I feel that this article, already too lengthy, leaves us still on the threshold of an immense subject. But if I have succeeded in making it clear that all resurrection is a giving back of bodily life, in contradistinction to the spiritual principle and the material elements, I shall think well of my efforts.

---

9   Ferrariensis, lib. IV, cap. 81

Man's soul is in a peculiar position with regard to the bodily resurrection, because it has a privileged condition, at least in the case of those who die in God's grace. Such souls have a wonderful existence, anyhow since Christ's ascension to heaven, and the additional privilege of the resurrection seems to add but little to man's happiness. Through Christ's death the state of death has been profoundly altered for the departed human spirit, if that spirit be a sanctified spirit. Yet even with the elect it is simply true to say that there is no true life except through the resurrection. In every condition, whether natural or supernatural, whether mortal or glorified, the normal state of the human soul is to be in the center of a life which is not spirit activity but sense activity. Outside that setting the human soul is far from being complete in its scope. Left to itself, without supernatural gifts of light and charity, the disembodied human spirit, imperishable through its very spirituality, is indeed a spirit in prison. The power of acting freely and congenitally comes to the human spirit in virtue of its union with sense life, and disembodiment, outside the privileged order of grace, far from meaning liberty to the spirit, means curtailment of its activities.

Catholic theology, based on St. Paul's doctrine of the spiritual body for the elect, in 1 Cor 15, is full of the glorious transformation of the life of the elect at the general resurrection. None of these awaitings of a spiritual, a heavenly body, are a denial of my main contention that resurrection is essentially the restoration of the life that has once been. The glorious bodily life of the elect is truly their old life, when their members served justice and sanctification, given back to them again:

> For as you have yielded your members to serve uncleanness and iniquity, unto iniquity: so now yield your members to serve justice, unto sanctification (ROM 6:19).

The glorious bodily life of the risen state is very much the restoration of that life of sanctity which made of a man's mortal body the temple of the Holy Ghost in the days of mortality. This is why in the classical presentment of Christianity resurrection from the dead is the whole range of the final reward.

For Christ, for St. Paul, resurrection from the dead is not one of the supernatural privileges, but it is the whole crown of heavenly reward:

> But they that shall be accounted worthy of that world and of the resurrection of the dead shall neither be married nor take wives. Neither can they die any more: for they are equal to the angels and are the children of God, being the children of the resurrection (LUKE 20:35-36).

> That I may know him and the power of his resurrection and the fellowship of his sufferings: being made conformable to his death, if by any means I may attain to the resurrection which is from the dead (PHIL 3:10-11).

The holy human life, interrupted by death, is restored with all its sanctities out of the storehouse of divine omnipotence, but without any of the limitations of mortality, and with the addition of qualities which in no wise interfere with its radical and substantial sameness.

The resurrection trump is God's peremptory command to the immense human army to be again as they were before, and "they that hear shall live" (JOHN 5:25), live as they had lived. It is not in the least necessary to hold that supernatural grace clings to the material elements. God's command to the life that has been, to be again what it had been, is the power that makes every detail of my present existence of immense value. What I do now, what I am now, what my life is now, will be bidden by God to show itself again, to exist again, "for he is not the God of the dead, but of the living: for all live to him" (LUKE 20:38).

I feel no mission here to make capital out of the Catholic tradition about the perfection of the risen body after the general resurrection, in favor of the possibility of a bodily resurrection. Resurrection ought to be considered by us as a thing possible to God under any circumstances, not merely under the privileged circumstances of the supernatural state. It is God's power to raise up any dead man for any object that His mercy or justice or general providence may have in view. We have first to believe in the bodily resurrection of members of Christ; the rising again of the reprobate has no special difficulty. If it had seemed good to the Son of God, in the days of His ministry, to raise from the dead one of His inveterate enemies, for some lofty purpose of His own, the dead man would have been raised up in the state of sin in which he had died. The same applies to the last resurrection.

Dr. Major evidently finds fault with the Catholic faith in bodily resurrection on aesthetical grounds. He brackets "Roman Catholics" and Mohammedans together, no doubt on the ground of a common coarseness of belief: "How could a refined man want a body to be happy in?" seems the contention of this evidently prosperous man.[10] The common answer to such superciliousness is to recapitulate from our catechism the qualities of the risen body, which certainly ought to satisfy any man whose spiritual ambition it is to become a beam of sunlight. This is making our pearls cheap. I think a recommendation for a little more sincerity in psychology would be more to the point.

Has Dr. Major, or anyone else on earth, ever known what it is to be without a body, without bodily life? What are we doing, when we become idealists, but projecting into eternity the experience of our bodily life? We know as little how it feels to be a spirit as we are ignorant of the sensation that would be ours if we were to contemplate the earth from the moon. Dr. Major's concluding words are:

It is this that I have done in stating publicly that the form which the doctrine of the resurrection assumes in my mind is the survival of death by a personality which has shed its physical integument forever. By survival, I need hardly add that I mean full survival of all that constitutes whatever is essential to a human personality; in short, all that is meant by the term "personal identity."[11]

10   Major, *Resurrection of Relics*, p. 90
11   Major, *Resurrection of Relics*, p. 90

Really, really! If Dr. Major asks for all that which constitutes his "personal identity " to appear again on the last day, and this even without any "physical integuments," his faith in God's creative power leaves the poor "Roman Catholic," and even the benighted Mohammedan, far behind. They never hoped for anything nor feared anything except that God would make them one day again what they are now, whilst Dr. Major's faith rises to the sublime height of expecting God to make him again one day what now he is not.

The defenders of the dogma of resurrection have pressed into service all the marvels of visible nature, with its endless vitalities, as possible illustrations of this one supreme marvel, the revival of the dead. The earlier Fathers, and notably St. Augustine, had recourse to an example from nature which is not often made use of now, but which is certainly very telling and interesting. Why should not the human race live again? Look at what happens on this earth. There is today living on our planet an immense multitude of men of whom not one was alive, say, twelve decades ago. Countless millions may be inhabiting this globe one day, and none of them is here today. Why, then, should it be impossible for God to people again this earth with all the men who no longer are? Such is in my phrase the patristic simile.

It will be said that there is not the least parity; as the existence of the future generations, however numerous, is precontained in the vitalities of the generation now living, whilst the renewed existence of all the dead is not precontained in anything here on earth. But it is here that the force of the patristic comparison becomes apparent. Whatever a creature or a set of creatures can do, God can do more perfectly. Creatures are the secondary causalities, God is the primary causality; now the primary causality can do in a more excellent way all the work of all the secondary causalities put together. All those future generations which will spring from the present generation through the laws of heredity, God could, if He so wished, create directly, with all the vitalities and characteristics that will be theirs through heredity. In other words, He could create, or make directly, all the men to whom present humanity will be the parent in the ordinary course of nature. And what God can do for the future, for the human beings who are not yet, He can do likewise for the past, for the human beings that no longer are.

What the natural human power of generation has produced—*i.e.* the past human race—has been the prey of death. Secondary causality, created causality, has had its day. But primary causality, God's causality, has not operated yet directly; it is still intact; it can do now what it could always do—*viz.*, put on this earth the innumerable lives that sprang from the first parents. So, on the day of the general resurrection this infinite reserve power will come into full play.

This working out of the ancient metaphor is, of course, my own; but I think that everyone will admit that it contains the germs of a great idea, the idea that God has the power to produce in an instant all that immense created life of sense, thought, and affection which it takes humanity the aeons of history to produce through natural development and evolution. And to be more precise, whatever is my own share in the building up of my own life, in the progressive ripening of my own personality, God can achieve in the twinkling of an eye.

May I then, as a final contribution to our great subject, the resurrection of the body, exhort my reader to undertake the refreshing task of studying all that is said in the Gospel of St. John on life and resurrection, in the light of all that has been written here?

I feel confident that Christ's constant reiteration in the Fourth Gospel that He has the power to give life, and more life, will then be clothed with a new radiance; and the discourses of Christ on life, on the food of life, on His desire to give Himself as our meat and drink in order that He may raise us up at the last day, will have a literalness which is as startling as it is logical:

Now this is the will of the Father who sent me: that of all that he hath given me, I should lose nothing; but should raise it up again in the last day. And this is the will of my Father that sent me: that everyone who seeth the Son and believeth in him may have life everlasting. And I will raise him up in the last day. ... He that eateth my flesh and drinketh my blood hath everlasting life: and I will raise him up in the last day (JOHN 6:39-40, 50).

What more can we desire? The Son of God is resolved "to lose nothing." In our bodies we receive His Body. It is the most beautiful intermingling of the heavenly and the earthly; it is bodily life at its highest, its best. Such a thing cannot be lost; He will raise it up again in the last day.

CPSIA information can be obtained
at www.ICGtesting.com
Printed in the USA
LVHW010839290122
709475LV00005B/682

9 780692 259023